1119

MIRACLE MAN

100 Days with Oliver

All the Best

&

Oliver

MIRACLE MAN

100 Days with Oliver

Robert B. Haas

Bascom Hill Publishing Group
MINNEAPOLIS, MN

Bascom Hill
Publishing Group

Bascom Hill Publishing Group

212 3rd Avenue North, Suite 290

Minneapolis, MN 55401

612.455.2293

www.bascomhillpublishing.com

ISBN - 1-935098-44-6

ISBN - 978-1-935098-44-7

LCCN - 2010913229

Cover Images by Robert B. Haas

Cover Design by Alan Pranke

Typeset by Sophie Chi

Printed in the United States of America

*This book is dedicated to the members
of Oliver's extended clan: two-leggers Candice,
Samantha, Courtney, Vanessa, and Gavin; and
four-leggers Elmer, Chloe, Henry, Spencer,
Cooper, Benny, Barkley, and Bosley.*

ACKNOWLEDGMENTS

From the Author:

I wish to thank my editor extraordinaire Rebecca Ascher-Walsh, who recognized that the true story of the Miracle Man could only be told by examining both ends of the leash, and who cajoled and coaxed that story out of my pen. Without Rebecca's rare gifts of insight and expertise, I would never have done justice to Oliver's struggles and to his emergence as the Miracle Man.

From Oliver:

Mark Twain once said, "It's not the size of the dog in the fight, it's the size of the fight in the dog." I wish to thank all the people in my life who recognized that inside the body of this fourteen-year-old, twenty-pound dog lurked the spirit of a fighter who intended to fulfill the promise of one hundred days: Dr. Julie Ducote, Dr. Emi Hayashi, and the entire staff at the North Texas Emergency Pet Clinic; Dr. Hugh Hays and his devoted staff at Summertree Animal Clinic; Dr. Lisa Newell of Malibu Coast Animal Clinic; and my therapists at the North Texas Animal Rehabilitation Center, Jennie Ralph and Rich Mysliwiec.

When we do the best we can, we never know what miracle is wrought in our life, or in the life of another.

—Helen Keller

Introduction

A Blindside Hit

JUST A FEW MONTHS AGO, MY WHOLE WORLD WAS rattled, its axis visibly wobbled. My best friend Oliver—a fourteen-year-old mixed breed that we rescued as a puppy from a no-kill shelter—tumbled down an embankment at our mountain retreat in California and never regained his footing, instantly paralyzed in his hind quarters. Ollie's medical history was already complex, to say the least—having suffered two nearly lethal bouts with a rogue immune system that attacked first the clotting agents in his blood and then his neuromuscular connections. In the past year, rapidly advancing cataracts had left him almost completely blind.

But Oliver is one tough guy. Weighing in at only twenty pounds, our boy had managed to stave off his own traitorous immune system with enough steroids to disqualify him from the Baseball Hall of Fame. And Ollie had learned that his eyes were not the most critical connection to his brain or his quality of life. He had adjusted well to Hamlet's oft-quoted description of life as the "thousand natural shocks that flesh is heir to" and had entered canine old age with a certain measure of dignity and class.

This time was different, however. We rushed Oliver back to our home in Dallas, only to discover that the paralysis had become the least of our problems, as Ollie was also diagnosed with pyothorax (an often fatal lung disease) as well as what was suspected to be cancer in his chest. In the brief span of a few days, things went from bad to worse to the unthinkable. Oliver was catapulting down a medical abyss, and I was tumbling with him. While I knew full well that Ollie was approaching the last phase of a long life, I had always assumed that his final days would be just as graceful and dignified as the rest of his life had been. I never imagined that the end would come in a rush of trauma and disease that seemed to be spinning out of control. I was caught totally off guard by this blindside hit.

Soon I was shuttling back and forth twice a day between our home and the veterinary intensive care unit, praying for "just" paralysis in his hind legs. I was prepared to exchange permanent paralysis for short-term survival, if only there were some way that I could close the deal on this compromise—a final hurdle that rarely eluded me in my life as a businessman. But that deal wasn't on the table. Instead, I heard words like "cremation" and "the merciful thing to do" in conferences where the vets dragged out the time-worn adage that I should "hope for the best, but prepare for the worst." I was even down to the point of walking our property in search of a final resting place for the boy we fondly referred to as our clan leader. The first in a progression of six canines that eventually arrived on the scene, Oliver was a natural alpha, bonding first to his two human parents—the ultimate alpha male and female—and never relinquishing his leadership position to any of the five younger canines that we assembled around him over the years.

Once Oliver had been absent for a few days during his stay in intensive care, our other dogs began to move in somewhat erratic and undisciplined directions, as if the steering column of a five-wheeled vehicle had come unhinged and the tires just rolled off in random directions unconnected to one another. The normal rhythm and melody of the clan was disrupted and cacophonous, resembling a collection of orchestral instruments warming up before that moment of silence when the maestro finally takes the podium, baton in hand. Oliver's first lieutenant Elmer (age thirteen) was particularly lost without his only older brother. Elmer and Oliver were exceptionally devoted to each other, usually napping in the same dog bed lying back to back, just barely touching along their spines but comforted by the warmth of each other's bodies. Without Oliver to lean on, Elmer paced around endlessly, aware that something was amiss; Oliver had simply been gone too long. And my sense of things being off kilter was palpable as well: I was obsessed with the thought of losing Oliver at any moment. Dogs are incredibly adept at sensing a shift in their master's moods, and I have no doubt that I was emitting to the clan a profound sense of angst in a silent language that was clearly understood by all.

Oliver was not the only member of the family who had been through the revolving door of an array of doctors' offices and hospitals. I had experienced my own labyrinth of medical tunnels: epileptic seizures, diagnosed brain cancer, heart disease, three operations to install a series of pacer-defibrillators in my chest, and hundreds of episodes of atrial fibrillation. But I had always managed to emerge from the tunnel and, in the process, had eventually learned to accept the fact that death inevitably follows life. That is one of the few benefits of engaging in a series of health crises that pose the risk of an "untimely" death. Once I had survived the first battle and then another one or two, I became a bit more philosophical—some might even say cocky—about meeting that dragon the next time around. And sure enough, there was always another time around. After a while, I began to think not in terms of avoiding death but rather of experiencing a good death—an exit that was postponed long enough to be "well-timed" and one that was shielded from the more gruesome declines that may ravage our bodies or rob our minds on the way out.

In an effort to stave off the panic that might otherwise have engulfed my family in the midst of one of my medical battles, I learned how to remain calm and strong—or at the very least how to do a good imitation of someone who was calm and strong. I refused to allow a sense of dread to seep out of my pores and infect my wife, Candice, or any of our three daughters. I was always the strong one, but I was never my own best friend . . . Oliver was my best friend.

The bond between a man and his dog has often been described as unconditional, as if the absence of conditions is at the heart of what distinguishes this love from any other. But *unconditional* is not exactly the right word, at least not in the case of my bond with Oliver. The right word is *uncomplicated*. It is a very straightforward, simple, and pure form of love. It does not grow burrs or calluses along the edges as time marches on. It does not, as with most marriages and other family bonds, go through stages with sharp-elbowed curves or periods of "growing apart" and later needing to reunite, in much the same way that a pair of skaters drifts apart to perform at opposite ends of the rink, only to return in sync with each other's cadence. Ollie and I were not as elegant as skaters—we were walkers, side-by-side, around a lake or at the ocean's edge, separated by only a few feet and always moving in the same direction and at the same pace.

From the very first moment that we rescued Oliver from the shelter, I began to knit together the tapestry of our relationship—and the thread was much thicker than the adorable antics that any three-month-old puppy uses to entice its new master into a state of rapture. It was indeed "love at first sight," the only form of love that I have ever known. Oliver and his littermates were scampering inside a pet store that was holding Adoption Day for foundlings from a nearby shelter, when Candice and our youngest daughter, Vanessa, walked in, intent on rescuing a puppy. Within a few minutes of receiving a call from Candice, I rushed over to the pet store to see the object of their newfound affections. As soon as I walked in, I laid eyes on this almost all black puppy with a white goatee and two white socks. Oliver lifted his eyes up at me, displaying white rims below, and you might as well have flashed a neon sign that blinked "Game Over!" I tied a red ribbon around his neck, signifying that this merchandise was no longer for sale, and stayed behind while Candice and Vanessa checked out a few more shelters despite my admonition that the search was officially over. Within an hour, I received another call from the Haas women, this time accepting surrender, and the soon-to-be-named Oliver was ours. Sixty dollars in cold cash sealed the deal, and at that instant Oliver became my first son, a position that would be his forever.

Even as a youngster, Oliver was a very serious guy. Being born into homelessness in the parking lot of an abandoned apartment building will have that effect on you. Not having a place to call home is a subject I know something about. My own homelessness was self-imposed, opting to escape during high school from an oppressive parental regime, drifting into an eleven-dollar-per-week boarding house populated with men more than three times my age. My fellow boarders were a grizzled lot who did not seem to own a razor between them, reminiscent of sepia images of Depression-era characters in bread lines. I doubt that Ollie's brief period of homelessness left quite as much scar tissue as mine. While his was involuntary, it was at an age when memory is hardly able to retain any vestige of hardship—and his ordeal was softened by the attentions of a remarkably caring mother and warm, wriggling siblings never more than a few inches or a few minutes away.

Ollie and I both emerged from our youth not only as serious characters but as cautious and suspicious ones as well. One of the things I always loved about Oliver was the fact that each stranger had to prove himself first, well before a wagging tail or licking tongue would signal that the test had been passed. Always quick to anger and slow to trust, Ollie held his affection in reserve until it was earned. And I was the same, at least until the last two decades of my life lengthened the fuse of my temper, a process we call mellowing. But the slow-to-trust part has remained just as acute as ever, perhaps even more so. The visible accumulation of material things has a way of attracting others—it's as if the newspaper clippings that trumpet your good fortune were injected with a hidden magnet that draws others in, and you are left with the unenviable task of separating those who would be drawn in anyway for the pleasure of your company from those who are drawn in by the size of your companies.

Sometimes it seems as if the only safe way to navigate is to assume that no one is drawn in without expectations, without complications. Eventually you weary of the task of separating the wheat from the chaff and conclude that perhaps it's just simpler not to allow newcomers to progress beyond the stage of casual acquaintance into the more risky zone of friendship.

But such was not the case with Oliver—Ollie never expected anything from me other than what almost anyone else could provide. His love was never infected with ulterior motives, and it did not ratchet up or scale down based on fluctuations in the Dow Jones Industrial Average. Ollie could never tell whether my latest deal or photo exhibit was heralded in a newspaper or magazine article that day. His blasé attitude toward newspaper clippings was reminiscent of the advice from my long-deceased but beloved Grandpa Arthur, who wagged his bony finger in my face at the start of my investment career and admonished me never to forget that yesterday's newspaper was used to wrap fish.

As the eventual leader of a troop of five other dogs that followed in his paw-prints, Oliver also understood that leadership is a lonely occupation. By its very nature, it does not allow for substitutes or peers who may step in and take your place when conditions toughen or exhaustion sets in; it is at those very moments that leadership is most cherished and most needed. In the wild, clan leaders are constantly "eye-balled" by their followers, who study their every move to detect any evidence of slippage, any sign that the leader may no longer be capable of sitting on the throne and ferreting out sustenance or protecting against danger. Born leaders such as Oliver develop a certain mental toughness, a self-dependency that wards off all manner of threats.

Despite his narrow, sloping shoulders, Oliver always wore the mantle of clan leadership well. This natural affinity for leadership, laced through with a hint of the melancholy that is often its companion, attracted me to him. Whenever we were together without anyone else around, the tension eased from both our shoulders—there was no clan or investment firm to lead. We could just walk together or sit together or lie together as kindred spirits without any expectations on either side. At such times, we were not master and pet—we were best friends. I talked to Oliver just the way I would talk to a person—and it mattered not a bit that Ollie did not understand my exact words. What he could understand was my tone and the affection for him that tone conveyed. In Oliver, I had found someone in whom I could confide—without reservation or any expectation of a retort. I had found someone who realized in his own way that while the weight of leadership tugs at your shoulders, in the end you know no other way and would never be content without that albatross around your neck.

During his first few days in the intensive care unit (ICU), Oliver and I hardly recognized each other. His eyelids barely opened beyond narrow slits and his ears lifted only slightly at the sound of my voice. And for my part, I did not remember a time when I could not reach out to him and receive a hearty dose of affection in return. Even during the near deadly duels with his rogue immune system, Ollie was always alert and aware of his circumstances. His twenty-pound body was never this limp, this lifeless.

Oliver was slipping away, and I was coming unhinged. I realized that if I lost him now, I would lose one of the ropes that fastened me to my moorings. I had invested so much of my love and friendship in this fellow but had never been prepared to harvest that investment when our time together was over. I blamed myself for being too cavalier in assuming that the end would be ever so gradual, allowing for a graceful exit, with perhaps a few curtain calls to thunderous ovations.

When Oliver was at his very lowest point in ICU, I still had faith in him, but the realities of his medical trauma were closing in on this fourteen-year-old guy. I literally prayed for just one hundred more days with Oliver, one hundred days of relatively pain-free time to spend with him, one hundred days to weave together as many memories as I could cram into that window of opportunity. I usually think in round numbers, perhaps a legacy of several decades in the investment business—thirty seemed far too brief and three hundred too greedy . . . one hundred seemed about the right place for a bargain, particularly since I was not exactly negotiating from a position of strength. Back then, when Candice and I slept with a cell phone next to our bed and had an understanding with the emergency night shift that "no news was good news," I dreaded the prospect of hearing that phone ring in the middle of the night. If it had, I would have been cheated out of the full measure of what I thought was a fair bargain—just one hundred days, that's all. But the phone never rang. In the end, I figured that Oliver would be the one to decide.

Quite often, fully baked thoughts enter my mind from somewhere, but I don't know where. It's almost as if the thoughts were inscribed on the wings of tiny paper airplanes that fly into my head from another zip code. More often than not, the thoughts are about a subject that I have been intensely focused on—a business deal or a photo project—but from which I have allowed myself a brief break in order to engage in a more mindless activity such as swimming laps. A few days into Ollie's hospital ordeal, as I was taking a shower one morning, one of those tiny paper airplanes flew into my ear with a message that Oliver would survive and would emerge from the ICU. I had no idea where that thought came from, but I didn't care—I believed it and that's all that mattered.

Soon afterward, something changed. I shook myself out of my stupor and Oliver did as well. After almost a week of being sedated and fed intravenously in an oxygen chamber, lying at the epicenter of a maze of tubes and dials and monitors, a visibly weakened Oliver started to rally back, to the slack-jawed amazement of his entire entourage of vet specialists and emergency techs. Twice daily deliveries of home-cooked boiled chicken pushed into his mouth began to take hold. His jaw went from being too weak to resist my finger pushing past his thin black lips to actually lunging at the scraps of shredded chicken once his sniffer confirmed that the next bundle was within striking distance. I obsessively followed the charts and graphs and numbers on the monitors that recorded his vital signs, not needing a medical degree to realize that we were at last headed in the right direction.

We all bore witness to the emergence of the fellow who would soon be known to all as the Miracle Man. One morning in the ICU, I bestowed his new name on him: "How's the Miracle Man doing?"…"Did the Miracle Man sleep well last night?"…"How was the Miracle Man's appetite today?" No one resisted the notion that Oliver deserved his new moniker; this nearly blind, partially paralyzed fourteen-year-old mixed breed was staging a remarkable comeback and had made believers of us all.

On the tenth day following his admission to ICU, all the tubes were disconnected, the last vestiges of supplemental oxygen were shut off, and Oliver was released to home care, still paralyzed in his rear extremities but most likely out of the proverbial woods. Oliver came out of ICU a noticeably frailer physical specimen, but with his dignity and intellect and spirit intact. But I was a different story. After emerging from a prolonged crisis, we sometimes allow ourselves the luxury of collapsing once the storm has been weathered—and this was such a time. I no longer felt the need to be strong for Ollie or Candice or our daughters, and it was only then that I realized just how vulnerable I was to the loss of Oliver.

Once I was no longer entangled in the day-to-day, hour-by-hour crisis that unfolded in ICU, I had time to reflect on the fact that I had almost lost my best friend, far sooner and more abruptly than I was prepared for. And what I needed most of all was time. I needed time to recover emotionally from clinging to the edge of the cliff, and time to savor the additional moments that had been tacked on to this life-and-death contest between Oliver and his body. I needed time to etch his lasting image and the contours of our relationship into a slab of marble. That marble would be a journal, and the chisel would be my pen. I promised myself that I would write a passage about Oliver on every one of those one hundred days, as both a memento of our time together and a tangible reminder that the extra days were to be cherished. I bargained for one hundred days, and that's what I needed. Anything less would not be enough.

The experience—both in ICU and in the days and weeks that followed—forced me to look inside my relationship with Oliver and deep inside myself. And so we began another journey together, Ollie and me, a journey of moments never again taken for granted—a journey of self-discovery with Oliver as the Miracle Man and the Professor, and me as his dedicated disciple. Oliver promised that the journey would last at least one hundred days—and Oliver always keeps his promises.

Chapter One

Setting the Stage

BY THE TIME OLIVER PRANCED ONTO THE STAGE as a three-month-old puppy in 1995, I was already looking to inject a fresh dose of drama into my life by exploring new professional frontiers. The investment world that I had inhabited for almost two decades had been exceedingly kind to me, but it was time to move on.

Following a brief stint in the 1970s as a corporate lawyer with a Midwest firm, the launch of my investment career at the age of thirty-one had been a shaky one, to say the least. The first six years were spent in the venture capital field with a small Ohio-based fund, learning the ropes as a thoroughly befuddled newcomer to the business. The conventional wisdom in the investment business is that you learn more from your worst deals than you do from your winners. If that's the case, then my first few years in the field were an uninterrupted sequence of education-rich experiences. The only major accomplishment that I managed to engineer during an otherwise forgettable tenure was an upgrade in my sartorial assets. Imitating the classic dress style of the senior partners of the firm, I actually began to look the part of a seasoned professional.

After a period of lackluster performance, I decided that it was time to transition to a different zip code in the business, literally and figuratively. Somehow the shores of Lake Erie did not seem to be the ideal locale for enhancing either my prospects as an investor or the vibrancy of my personal life. So I gathered up Candice and our three young daughters—Samantha (age eleven), Courtney (nine), and Vanessa (two)—and followed the wise counsel of Horace Greeley ("go west, young man") to seek my fortune in more fertile climes—southwest to be more accurate and Dallas to be exact.

In 1983, I joined up with another fellow in the investment business who was also waiting for divine providence to smile down upon him, and we formed the Dallas firm "Hicks & Haas" as an early entrant into the brand-new field of leveraged buyouts. Armed to the teeth with Texas-sized swagger and groundless self-confidence, we crafted a game plan that could best be described as somewhere between audacious and foolhardy. It was our stated intent to buy one company after another even though we had virtually no track record, barely enough capital to pay the utility bills on our spartan offices, and near total dependence on the backing of institutional capital from the canyons of Wall Street. But this was the Oklahoma land rush days of the leveraged buyout (or

LBO) business—all you needed was a six-shooter, a covered wagon, and a team of freshly watered horses.

As luck would have it, it turned out to be the perfect time to enter the LBO business, before the competition was fierce and the vultures swept in. Over the next few years, we corralled a sequence of deals that changed my life forever. In a mind-numbing blitzkrieg of transactions within the span of just over three years, Hicks & Haas managed to cobble together the third largest soft drink conglomerate in U.S. history behind only Coke and Pepsi, with our acquisitions of Dr Pepper, 7-Up, A&W, Welch's, Squirt, Vernors, Country Time Lemonade, and other small niche brands—not to mention a handful of healthcare and industrial concerns with names that were not nearly as recognizable but whose values were just as enticing. It was the psychedelic days of the early LBO era, when galloping ambition and hard-nosed reality occasionally bumped into each other to the everlasting delight of those few among us who just happened to be in the right place at the right time.

By the late 1980s, at the age of forty-one, I had a chance to head to the pay window, cash in my chips, walk through the door marked EXIT, and never look back. And that was an opportunity I had no intention of passing up. Even though I had bolted from the family residence when I was only sixteen, I had taken with me more than a few pairs of jeans and a couple of T-shirts. I had also taken along my father's sense of raw ambition and his admonition that I should never settle for anything less than being the best at whatever I chose to do in life. It was a weighty yoke to lay around the neck of a kid who was still figuring out how to deal with puberty. But it was also a compass that was designed to adjust my sights upward from what could readily be achieved to what could hardly be imagined. And while I chafed under his harsh regime, I also watched him carefully and knew him to be a shrewd businessman who had an uncanny sense of timing. I may have rejected the heavy-handed man who was my father, but I had enough sense to realize that the same man saw potential that was either mine to fulfill or mine to squander.

After only a handful of years in the LBO business, it was time to realize that potential and assuage that raw ambition. The leveraged buyout arena is a treacherous field in which to practice the art of investing. In the jargon of war, it is a landscape littered with IEDs and booby-traps for the naive or the arrogant who believe in their own Midas touch. Even though I had only served a brief stint in that war zone, I felt like a grizzled combat veteran who had repeatedly walked back and forth across a minefield and then looked down to discover that there were still ten toes attached to my feet and all ten fingers attached to my outstretched arms. I knew better than to believe all the newspaper and magazine clippings that trumpeted our investment savvy—I was fully aware of the fact that the past decade had turned into a delicious brew composed of a measure of intense labor, a pinch of strategic thinking, and a boatload of incredible luck.

Even though the ground beneath my feet was spinning, I remembered well the wise counsel of a veteran Texas investor who once draped his arm across my shoulder and whispered in my ear in a distinct Southern drawl, "Bobby boy, if you ever get the chance to put on a bullet-proof vest, then you put it on, and never take it off." Over the next few years, we sold the vast bulk of our portfolio at the nose-bleed prices that were not uncommon in that era. Virtually all our soft drink holdings ultimately found a new home as part of the Cadbury-Schweppes juggernaut of consumer products companies.

After a glorious sprint across the rugged landscape of the investment world, my partner and I disbanded Hicks & Haas, content at that point to follow separate paths. Once I had deposited the bulk of my winnings in gilt-edged, low-risk bonds that offered none of the thrill of the LBO business but all of the comfort of a warm, fuzzy blanket, I gingerly walked back into the business and stepped up to the poker table once again—but this time risking only a small portion of the chips that I had scraped off the table just a year or so before. In the spirit of the famed "Peanuts" comic strip, I was the character Linus—philosophical, but always clinging to his security blanket. Over the ensuing years, I continued to play the LBO game (and still do to this day), salting away my winnings whenever Lady Luck paid a return visit, and offering homage to our occasional bad deals as not-so-gentle reminders of how it could all evaporate in a heartbeat if you elected to risk too much or stay too long.

Somehow in the midst of all the heady changes, I came to grips with the fact that such outsized rewards were earned but not deserved. The rewards were certainly earned in the sense that we did not inherit a single nickel, and anyone else in the investment business was free to pursue the same bold strategy that we had. But our payback wasn't deserved, in the same sense that a third baseman doesn't deserve $25 million per year for hitting a baseball and an actor doesn't deserve $20 million for a few months' work. None of us had discovered a cure for a devastating disease nor had we negotiated a cease-fire to a bloody civil war. We were simply playing in an arena that, for whatever reason, bestowed princely sums on the few who did succeed.

When I pulled my chips off the table, I didn't have the foggiest idea that just a few years later (and, once again, in recent times), the financial world would be rocked by earthquakes that would leave carefully assembled fortunes in shambles. I just knew where I came from—I remembered well the eleven-dollar-per-week boarding house that became my den in high school and the three years at law school when Candice would buy extra cartons of milk whenever it was on sale. I was always afraid of "losing it all" and was convinced that if I did, I would never be able to duplicate what had been accumulated in the first place.

As welcome as the results of my first decade in the LBO business may have been, the frantic pace at which events unfolded had never been part of my original calculus. A game plan that was supposed to achieve financial security over a period of thirty years or so had unfolded at warp speed. In the span of just a few years, my carefully planned future was clearly visible in the rear-view mirror. That warp speed has a way of bending not only time but also your mind. Perhaps I was never prepared to accept failure, but I was also ill-equipped to encounter Lady Fortune so soon. Even though a bit disoriented, I at least knew enough to sit down and wait until I had my bearings before launching into any new ventures.

Once the carousel began to slow down, I was able to focus on other aspects of my life. And when I looked around, I found that all the riches that one could possibly imagine were already at my feet: a marriage of more than twenty years to my childhood sweetheart, and our three beautiful daughters. It was time to restore the balance between business and family. Both of us knowing full well that I was hell-bent on seeking my fortune, Candice and I had struck an unspoken bargain many years before: if the quest played out as planned, we would all be the beneficiaries, but there would come a time to shift the balance back toward the personal side. The time had arrived, more abruptly than we ever thought possible, to honor the other side of the bargain.

As the business theater of my life calmed down, a good portion of the vacuum of time that was left in its wake was devoted to family. Eventually, Samantha and Courtney would head off to Harvard Law School and later be handed their diplomas by Dean Robert Clark, a classmate of mine from the Harvard Law class of '72. Vanessa would continue to soar over equestrian fences as a world-class competitor, ultimately representing the United States as the youngest member of the U.S. team at the World Cup in Leipzig, Germany, graduating two years later from my other alma mater, Yale.

But well before the Ivy schooling of my daughters had been completed, I began to feel restless, once again. I may have figured out a way to throttle back in the investment business, but the eye of the tiger had not grown dim—I needed to find a new outlet for the raw ambition that doesn't desert you so readily. It was time to establish a fresh set of goals for the journey forward. At first by accident and then by design, I chose to trade in my calculator for a camera. I began a fresh journey down a radically different road populated with artists and editors, a road that would lead to remote and mystical places I had hardly even heard of before. It was time to carve a new path—this time as a photographer—and Oliver was destined to be part of my life during that entire journey.

In 1994, at the age of forty-seven, I purchased my very first camera and headed for the wilds of Africa. The very simple point-and-shoot camera that I toted along on that first safari was almost an afterthought, a way to bring back a few souvenirs just in case I never returned to Africa again. But I was wholly unprepared for the effect that this exotic realm would have on me. In that once "dark continent," I found two loves that have never deserted me since—a love of wild animals and a love of wild places. Over the ensuing eight years, I would head back to Africa more than twenty times, carrying more and more sophisticated camera gear on each return engagement. The photography itself morphed from a hobby to a passion and eventually to a full-fledged career that sprouted its own set of goals—it was not long before the eye that looked through the viewfinder of the camera became the proverbial eye of the tiger.

In between photo safaris, Candice and I began to assemble a clan around Oliver—first Elmer, then Chloe (our only female and the only pure breed), and then a succession of cocka-poos and bichon-poos with such distinguished names as Henry Alexander, Spencer Benson, and Cooper Bradley. I found that all the emotion I had invested in Oliver could easily be replicated as more and more canines came on board. Soon the clan itself became another theater of my life. Like the distant shores of my photographic world, the clan offered up a pace and a simplicity that were a welcome relief from my frantic years in the investment business. The four-leggers drew me into a realm that was peopleless and uncomplicated and boyish, a no-strings-attached world in which nothing was expected of me.

Oliver always set the tempo of the clan, but each new member added a fresh element to the brew—Elmer's allegiance to his older brother and near-perfect behavior; Chloe's saucy female temperament inside a lovely petite body (an apt description of the other women in the Haas family); Henry's emerging alpha streak that often posed a challenge to Oliver's hegemony; Spencer's raw instinctual skills and incredible speed of foot; and Cooper's childish and plucky behavior as the spoiled baby of the clan.

But the realm of the clan was not one that I could inhabit at the same time that I plied my craft as a photographer—while Oliver and his mates were never far from my mind, our bodies were separated several times each year by the draw of more distant locales. I tucked a batch of photos of Ollie and the gang inside the main photo bag that was always at my side, and I often leafed through those images and smiled the silent smile of someone who longed for a return to his loved ones. Through a strange assortment of e-mail, cell phones, and land lines—and the last resort of a call-anywhere-from-anywhere Iridium satellite phone—I managed to stay in reasonable touch with the shenanigans of the clan from places whose communications networks were often as primitive as their landscapes were majestic.

After a few years of photo safaris, I began to entertain the notion that one day I might actually publish a few of my photos. National Geographic was never part of the equation—that is, until I met more and more photographers. Over the years, it became clear that the most widely held ambition in the world of photography is to have an image (just *one* image) published by National Geographic—and eventually I came to share that somewhat far-fetched ambition.

By 2002, I was specializing in aerial photography—despite an acute case of acrophobia when my feet were planted on the ground. For weeks at a time, I would hang out of the open sides of helicopters whose doors had been unhinged, capturing images in some of the most remote places on earth.

Taking wing in a helicopter was a notion that I hatched in Africa one afternoon simply as a way to gain a different perspective on the wild animals that I had been photographing from ground level for the past eight years—a literal flight of fancy that turned into something more. That first aerial excursion in 2002 over the Okavango Delta of Botswana changed everything—I somehow left my acrophobia on the ground and was instantly mesmerized by the view from above. I discovered that I was a totally different photographer up there—my eyes and my hands and my mind just seemed to work more in sync with each other. I instinctively knew what I wanted to do, where I wanted to point the camera, and how I wanted to frame the image.

While I had trepidations before that first flight, I soon welcomed the risk of being exposed to the elements with nothing connecting me to the chopper except a simple leather harness, and I relished the thought that there were only a few lunatics out there who were doing the same thing. I realized that there was an opportunity to become an artist whose images would not be crowded out of museums or exhibits by the work of masters from centuries or even decades ago. It was fresh artistic turf—like discovering a new continent to be captured on film. It was the photographic equivalent of the LBO days of the early 1980s—a world drenched in risk but dangling outsized rewards in front of the very few who dared to enter it.

After just a few flights, I knew that I had found my artistic niche—from that point on, I never took another ground-based photo trip. In 2003, my aerial work came to the attention of one of the senior executives at National Geographic, and I was invited back to its D.C. headquarters to do a presentation of my photographs. The collection of aerial images captured the fancy of the folks at Nat Geo, and we undertook to do a pan-Africa book of aerial images that was ultimately published in seventeen languages under the title *Through the Eyes of the Gods: An Aerial Vision of Africa.*

By this time, our daughters were on the East Coast at law school and college. As a result, my well-wishers upon departure on a photo excursion—and the greeters upon my return—had changed from Candice and our daughters to Candice and Oliver's clan. Once I was safely back in the States, the clan never seemed to mind the fact that my outfits and duffel bags carried the strange scents of unknown species from across the ocean. The minute I walked in the house, I was licked and sniffed and nuzzled into submission by a passel of furry bodies. Candice preferred to withhold her more effusive displays of affection until after a prolonged shower and a fresh shave had proven beyond a shadow of a doubt that the grubby alien who had walked through the door was in fact her husband.

Fresh on the heels of the unexpected acclaim that the Africa book enjoyed, Nat Geo and I decided that I would canvas the length and breadth of Latin America. Soon I was hanging out of helicopters for another two years, soaring above exotic sites from the Rio Grande in the north all the way to the Strait of Magellan in the south. Once again, the resulting work (*Through the Eyes of the Condor: An Aerial Vision of Latin America*) found its way into seventeen languages—and then it was time to tackle another continent or two.

Emboldened by having "conquered" my fear of heights over the African savanna and the spine of the Andes, I decided to take on my fear of the cold—and what ensued was a four-year project that spanned the Arctic from Scandinavia to Iceland to Greenland to North America, ultimately emerging as my third aerial book, titled *Through the Eyes of the Vikings: An Aerial Vision of Arctic Lands*. Perhaps I was intent on tempting fate by exposing myself first to the heights that taunted me and then to the cold that provoked a deep-seated fear of being stranded in a desolate place.

Unlike Africa or Latin America, the Arctic represented a zone that aroused both fear and admiration in the core of my psyche. I can't stand the cold. The mere mention of names such as "Greenland" or "Iceland" literally sends chills down the back of my arms. But somehow I was drawn to the romance and the challenge of facing the Arctic—a grossly mismatched duel where the best you can do is to escape unharmed and unbowed. And so I responded to the challenge—for four years, I retraced the icy footprints of the

Vikings, my mode of travel a helicopter and not the longboat of centuries past.

Eventually, my dream of having "just one image" published by National Geographic blossomed into a series of multiyear book projects that covered the globe, with exhibits and publications in places I had never imagined I would set foot upon. I had managed to transform myself from an LBO artist to an artist-artist.

The high-wire world of Wall Street and the acrobatics of aerial photography in remote locales take place in radically different arenas: one transpires in a venue that is crowded with bodies and outsized egos where money is the only "coin of the realm," and the other takes place in faraway places that sometimes have no name at all and are populated by creatures that have rarely, if ever, set eye upon a human being before.

With the benefit of hindsight, I find it strange how life reveals itself in brief truncated strips. In more youthful times, I was seduced into a single-minded search for fame and gold. With pumping arms and legs, I joined the chase—oblivious to where the constant motion might all lead, vaguely sensing that there must be some point to all the sweat and toil.

In time, I was able to afford the luxury of pausing—to take stock of covered ground and miles past. The hot pursuit of worldly goods brought its own rewards along the way—but better yet, it printed a currency that allowed the march to halt and choose another path. This new journey led far away from the beaten track—to the Okavango Delta's vast expanse with thundering herds, and glacial paths with solitary travelers. In places with exotic names like Skeleton Coast and Kosi Bay, contentment cast its spell on me, in timeless rhythms barely known to modern ears. In a note of exquisite irony, the course that lay ahead for me reached back to lands still lingering behind.

It is strange in retrospect just how perfectly the timing of Oliver's entry onto the stage of my life coincided with this transition to the realm of wilderness photography. My life with Oliver and my career as a photographic artist unfolded on parallel tracks in uncanny balance with each other.

In the course of just a year or so after his adoption, Oliver became my best friend. Once you become my friend, you stand an excellent chance of becoming my best friend—the competition for the top slot has never been very crowded. I emerged from childhood with a high level of cautiousness about people and relationships and a tendency not to count on others for approval. Trust was a precious commodity in my world, to be parsed out carefully and in small doses. In contrast with the people from my childhood, Oliver exhibited all the fidelity of spirit and constancy of emotion that would form the mortar of a solid friendship—guile and treachery were not among his portfolio of traits. Once you were part of his inner circle, there was nothing to fear at all—your trust in him, and his in you, would never be betrayed.

Over the entire span of Oliver's life, I ping-ponged back and forth between the realms of business and photography and ultimately found peace and serenity only in the one—and for reasons that have drawn me closer and closer to Oliver and his five clan mates. The special brand of contentment that I found among the desert sweep of Namibia and the towering glaciers of Greenland resonated inside a psyche that had already discovered the beauty of my intensely personal relationship with Oliver. Like the distant locales where I practiced my photographic trade, my love of Oliver offered up raw simplicity and exquisite charm. Our time together had become every bit as cerebral as it was physical—resting his head in the crook of my arm when I slept, lying patiently along the edge of the pool as I swam my endless laps, or simply strolling by my side when I retreated from the world.

There was no artifice in my love of remote places—and there was none in my love for Oliver. I did not need to speak when I inhaled the grandeur of the Andes—and I did not need to utter a single word when I exchanged glances with Oliver. I watched in awe when I witnessed the cheetahs of Africa survive against overwhelming odds in the life-and-death drama that unfolds every day in the savanna grasslands—and I felt no less respect for Oliver when I watched him cheat death in ICU and emerge from that oxygen chamber prepared to assume his rightful place as clan leader once again.

There was a steadiness and a reliability about my photographic pursuits that seemed to mirror the steadiness and reliability of my relationship with Oliver. And there was a sense of distance that pervaded each world. My enchantment with aerial photography clearly had something to do with the fact that the drama unfolded well above the surface of the earth and far away from civilization; it provided a fresh sense of perspective that only distance would allow. And my enchantment with Oliver had something to do with the fact that it offered breathing space from the intensity of my daily life—a measure of distance from an existence that was often overwrought with deadlines and projects and pressures.

With the passage of time, I began to appreciate the fact that, as with my love for Oliver, I was drawn to my photography by the "friendship" it represented. The companionship and the comfort that the cameras, the images, and the pristine venues offered up mirrored the qualities that I cherished most in my relationship with Oliver. Of course, there were differences between my love of photography and my love for my faithful companion. Cameras don't gaze into your eyes and exude a stream of affection coming back at you, and images don't snuggle up to you at night with their warm furry bodies. And you can't always count on your photography to meet your expectations. But I could always count on Oliver. What I learned in ICU, however, was that I could not count on him forever. But "forever" was not the bargain—the bargain was one hundred days.

Chapter Two

A Wobbly Start

Days 1-5

AN EPIC MARCH ACROSS A HARSH LANDSCAPE—
be it Africa or the Arctic or the winding road to recovery—is
a journey that should only be undertaken with a hefty supply
of patience in your saddlebags and a trusty compass in your
pocket. Patience is normally a commodity that I find to be in
short supply when I do a recon of my personal assets, but the
ability to stay on course is something that comes naturally to
me, particularly when I hit upon a mantra for a long journey.
And the mantra for this one-hundred-day march was simply
to *cherish today*. For the first day of the journey and for every
day that followed, that mantra served as a gentle reminder
that my limited time with Oliver was the bargain that was
struck with his indomitable spirit—no less than one hundred
days together; that was the deal. Since there were plenty of
moments in the ICU when no one was sure that Oliver would
ever rejoin his clan or return to his accustomed haunts, the

admonition—and the commitment—to cherish today was a message that would weave its way so deeply into the fabric of my daily life that it would no longer need repeating.

In the first few days after his emergence from intensive care, I decided that it would be best to work from home. But there was something surreal about sitting down at a computer and attempting to wade through the e-mails that had accumulated during the black hole of his hospital stay. I felt fragile, just as fragile as the gray and emaciated body of that fourteen-year-old guy who seemed to wile away his normal waking hours in deep sleep. Oliver was back but his strength was not, at least not yet. And I was thrilled to have him home, but my confidence was not back, at least not yet.

I was definitely still struggling—struggling from the exhaustion of his ten days in ICU, struggling to broaden the single-minded focus on Oliver simply living through another day, struggling to believe that life would ever be the same again. Those days in intensive care were spent in the dragon's cave with its fire-belching breath singeing my hair.

After the ten-day passage through ICU, I was about to start another march—this one of one hundred days' duration—and I felt as if there ought to have been a way station between the two treks, a plateau where we could take stock of the past and gaze into the future, recharge our batteries and replenish our supplies. But Oliver was given no such break, and neither was I.

Although I never thought I'd admit to this, in the first few days after his release, there was actually something I missed about ICU. The sterile ambience of the hospital was gone in one fell swoop, a world we left behind in a thirty-minute drive from the hospital parking lot to our home. At first, I actually missed the rigors—and the security—of intensive care. Trained technicians and vets were in attendance twenty-four hours a day, Oliver's monitors spewed out an endless stream of data that measured his vital signs, and his supplemental oxygen intake could be continuously calibrated to conform to his exact needs. But not anymore. Now we just had the regular house and the regular people who populated that house. The lifeline that had tethered Oliver to emergency care at a moment's notice had been cut, and I sensed that his life raft was drifting just a bit. My single-minded focus on Oliver's survival was trained on a new venue—I had never thought of our home as a triage facility, and somehow it all didn't fit together.

Even though Oliver was the one with the paralysis, I felt vulnerable and unsteady on my legs around him. I carefully watched his breathing to detect any sign that the labored respiration that signals pyothorax had crept back into his lungs. I frequently used a stethoscope to listen to his heart rate. I stared into his cloudy, cataract-filled eyes to see whether the flickers of life had grown brighter or dimmer since I had last checked.

Despite all the scraps of medical knowledge that I had collected in the course of my own and Oliver's travails, in the final analysis, all I could do was to shower Ollie with attention and affection and begin to restore some semblance of his prior life. His body was still sufficiently fragile that I only felt comfortable leaving him in the company of the most docile of his clan comrades—his loyal lieutenant Elmer—to avoid any injury from the normal roughhousing that ensues when boys will be boys. Except for Elmer, the clan leader was forced to extend still further his already extended leave-of-absence from his posse.

The process of simply addressing his normal bodily functions sprouted a whole new range of interactions between Oliver and the people in his life. Not yet strong enough to sit up through an entire feeding session with his head lowered over his bowl, Ollie had to be patiently hand-fed until sufficient sustenance had been taken in. Candice and I were forced to guess when Oliver was thirsty and carry him to his water, since there was no way for him to amble over to any of the strategically placed water bowls that were distributed all around the house.

And most important of all, we learned how to use a towel-assisted technique to raise his lower torso so that his meals and fluid intake could be expelled from his system. That ability to use the precious remnants of his strength to support himself on his front legs and to rid his body of what needed to exit through the back was critical to his survival and recovery. But thankfully, there was enough strength and enough control of his bowels and his bladder to do so. In the pre-paralysis days, Ollie rarely lingered when it was time to do his business—his no-bullshit attitude was something akin to *business is business . . . when it's time to do it, you just do it and mosey around afterward.* In this new phase of his life and to his utter surprise, I greeted each deposit of fresh fertilizer from his body with raucous applause and an occasional fist pump. When there is cause for celebration in something as mundane as the body's ability to purge itself, you realize that the mantra of cherishing today is definitely beginning to take hold.

I have always fashioned myself an optimist. To my way of thinking, the hallmark of a true optimist is that you always look forward to what is to be gained and not backward to dwell on what has been lost. The moment Oliver left the hospital was the last time I ever pined away for the days when our clan leader would scamper around our property and chase squirrels or walk along the edge of the wall that rimmed our duck-filled pond. From a physical point of view, I only focused on what could be gained from this point forward—what Oliver could do to restore the maximum measure of mobility in his life without taking further risk with a delicate fourteen-year-old body.

Somewhat to my surprise, we found ourselves in a city where the most advanced forms of physical rehab had trickled down from the facilities that treat humans to the ones that treat our four-legged brethren . . . and we were exceedingly fortunate to be in a position to spare no expense in taking full advantage of those facilities. After just a few days at home, it was time to take our first tentative steps on the road to recovery with Ollie's initial rehab session at the North Texas Animal Rehabilitation clinic. The lead therapist, Jennie, was as upbeat and vivacious as could be, and Oliver wasted no time in displaying all the charm and *joie de vivre* that had captured many a female heart along the way.

In addition to my being given careful instruction in a series of stretching exercises and massage techniques, Oliver was measured for a custom-fitted set of wheels that were designed to substitute for his back legs. The contraption consisted of two rubber wheels, an array of metal tubing, and soft nylon netting that would be harnessed onto his torso and hopefully restore a sense of four-point motion. It would be a few weeks before his wheels arrived and we learned whether Ollie would take to this new vehicle—but simply being fitted for one was a forward-looking undertaking.

It was also a very different emotional experience at the rehab clinic compared to the ICU, working with upbeat therapists who were focused only on our plans for the future. We were no longer preoccupied with mere survival. The exercise techniques and the placing of a rush order on the shiny new set of wheels seemed to be the first flag that we planted in the sand, declaring for all the world to hear that we were moving forward. While the edge of the cliff was only a few inches away, forward motion became the order of the day. We were among experts who had restored mobility to other four-leggers and who marveled at how well Ollie seemed to be doing just a few days into his post-discharge life.

During the session itself, we definitely felt a bit of resistance when Jennie and I took turns pushing his two rear legs back from the fully extended position toward his torso. His body was clearly sending a message that it had an inkling of what was happening back there. The toughness that is at the heart of this creature was talking back.

Ollie slept well that night after a momentous first day of rehab. And I slept better too for the first time since the accident that propelled him into emergency care. There was something new in our "cherish today" world—there was a sense that Oliver was moving forward.

In the first few days, my best friend was healing a bit better than I was. Ollie somehow seemed more prepared mentally to handle the pitfalls and the setbacks that would inevitably litter his journey along the road to recovery. From my photographic safaris across the savanna grasslands of Kenya to the tundra of the Arctic, I had witnessed firsthand, over and over again, how animals are equipped with an incredible array of restorative powers. Such is the heritage that canines have been blessed with from thousands of years ago as the descendants of their great wolf ancestors. Injury and illness were always fatal if a wolf did not figure out how to quickly rally back to life. There were no vets, no prescriptions, and virtually no margin for error for an injured wolf. For the creature in the wild, you either heal or you die. And somehow that message got imbedded in the canine DNA that had been passed down to Oliver over scores of generations.

Even during that first week at home, I sensed that Oliver was beginning the process of knitting his life back together one stitch at a time. There was a palpable sense that Ollie was *thinking* . . . thinking not so much about what had transpired but rather about how the challenges of his new regimen could be met. He seemed to be figuring things out—how to eat, what his new routines would be, how to conserve his strength.

But I was not doing nearly so well. While Candice shared my love for Oliver, she also realized that in my mind losing Oliver would have been a blow akin to losing a cherished member of the family. Candice was always there to comfort me—but I was somewhere else entirely and simply inconsolable. To my way of thinking, this was purely a binary calculus: either Oliver survived or he did not. My marriage partner of forty years understood only too well that we all bond differently to different people and different things, and that on the stage of my life—which contained fewer people than it did things—Oliver was a major player.

I felt as if I were obliged to focus all my energies on his recovery. During his stay in intensive care and for the first few days afterward, my near paramilitary regimen of regular meals, exercise, and sleep had been in a state of utter disarray. I had become totally reliant on my Blackberry to catch the falling knives of business urgencies that rained down, but I was neglecting my own body in favor of concentrating on Ollie's.

Finally, after almost two weeks of total absence, I returned to the office shortly after his inaugural rehab session in an effort to resume some semblance of a regular routine. On that first day back, even though I was receiving regular reports as to how his day was unfolding, my concentration was jarred off course. I seemed to be adrift in a world in which others were focusing and I was not. Conference calls about our investment portfolio and e-mails from my colleagues at National Geographic seemed to be taking place in an ancient dialect of English, in which you recognize some of the words but have difficulty following the meaning. The old office routines had lost their urgency, and the goal-oriented tempo that normally allowed for a frontal assault on my robust to-do list was reduced to a more lethargic pace.

We all heal differently from wounds. The peculiar ability of animals to live in the present moment is an exceedingly valuable asset at such times. Virtually no mental or physical energy is wasted gazing through the rear-view mirror. For me, the wound was so fresh and so deep that the process of knitting cleaved flesh back together again had not even begun.

Every evening for roughly the past twenty years, I had taken a rather heavy dose of the blood-thinning agent Coumadin to prevent clots from forming and coursing through my system in the event of a prolonged cardiac episode of atrial fibrillation. Despite the fact that those episodes are now quite rare, Coumadin has probably become a permanent part of my arsenal of medications. But with my blood watered down to the point that clots are highly unlikely, I am also susceptible to excessive bleeding, even from the nick of a shaving snafu. My ability to heal quickly from a wound has been compromised in exchange for a buffer of protection against a debilitating stroke. I don't heal as well as I used to, and I was not healing as well as Oliver from the wounds of the past two weeks.

For Oliver, Day 5 of his one-hundred-day journey was the equivalent of the one-mile mark of a twenty-six-mile marathon—only about five percent. It dawned on me that in many ways, this one-hundred-day journey was the exact opposite of a marathon run. In a marathon, runners start out fresh and strong and bursting with confidence, their batteries at full strength, their legs limber, their minds totally prepared to navigate the challenges ahead. But Oliver started this marathon almost totally depleted of physical strength. His limbs—front and back—could hardly be described as supple or strong. Strength and agility, if they were to come at all, needed to be fashioned and tooled along the way. Such improvements would be extracted from his body at a cost of straining with daily exercises and weekly therapy, and pushing himself up against "the wall" that marathoners describe as the image best fitting the last few miles of the race.

In our own version of the marathon, the fifth day was our first day of setback. Oliver stumbled, and I fell down. What turned out to be a minor reversal rattled my nerves and infected my mood with the goblins that I thought I had left behind in the ICU. On the plus side that day, Ollie did demonstrate some impressive upper-body strength, managing to scoot himself (with derrière down) across the bedroom floor in search of water. But even though Ollie's attitude and vital signs were steady, our boy vomited both his meals.

After the second episode of evening vomiting, I decided to take him downstairs and sleep with him in the kitchen the rest of the night, curled up on a love seat that is considerably shorter than my six-foot, one-inch frame (it might have been just right for Napoleon . . . *sans* Josephine). Candice and I agreed that she would remain behind and keep an eye on the other hounds who share our bed and whose slumber had been disrupted by the fire drill of cleaning up after Ollie's nausea. Downstairs, sleep only came in fitful teaspoon measures, so I busied myself checking his breathing and pulse repeatedly. In the morning, Ollie seemed more bright-eyed, his nose was cold, and his towel-assisted walk was reasonably vigorous.

I was not nearly so copacetic. After six hours of being scrunched up on the love seat, my limbs were exceedingly sore, and the past twenty-four hours had left me depleted. Despite all the progress to date, the slightest setback felt like a punch in the gut. I could feel every one of my sixty-two years as if each had been tattooed onto the canvas of my skin.

As the day wound down to a close, I realized that the essential ingredients for Oliver's marathon were exactly the same as for the twenty-six-milers—guts, mental toughness, and a strong instinct for survival. We were indeed in the midst of a marathon, and the one-mile mark was an achievement of sorts—but there were ninety-five days yet to go.

Chapter Three

The Miracle Man Emerges

Days 6-9

EVEN THOUGH THE SIXTH DAY AFTER ICU WAS A Sunday, once we contacted Oliver's regular vet, Dr. Hugh Hays, to report the episodes of repeat vomiting, Dr. Hays volunteered to rush in on his day off (a one-hour commute each way) to examine Ollie and see what might be causing the problem. The inability of such a weakened animal to retain any nourishment at all is a very serious matter, and Dr. Hays was not about to wait until Monday for an explanation. Having attended to Ollie ever since we adopted him fourteen years earlier, Dr. Hays knew this pup inside and out and had gained no small amount of respect for his ability to rebound several times before from life-threatening illnesses. Hugh and I had always had a healthy measure of respect for each other and a bit of career envy as well. I sometimes fantasized about being a vet on a white horse arriving just in the nick of time to save a creature's life from the brink of disaster, and

Hugh frequently offered to "carry my photo bags" on my next aerial adventure.

Upon examination, Oliver's vitals were fine, his temperature was normal, and his clinical behavior was "unremarkable" (a remarkable change from the past few weeks). Doc Hays confirmed my suspicion that Ollie's heavy and complex drug regimen had upset his stomach, but that it was no more serious than that.

Relieved to have a solid overall exam under our belt and armed with a credible explanation for his vomiting, we dashed home with Oliver riding shotgun. When we arrived, the entire troop afforded their clan leader the respect of their traditional welcoming ceremony—wagging tails, submissive whimpering, and muzzle-to-muzzle brushes. Afterward, Ollie enjoyed a leisurely bath, followed by two home exercise sessions, and a laid-back afternoon soaking up human embraces and messages of affection that Candice and I whispered in his drooping ears.

For the first time since his release from ICU, I felt noticeably buoyed. Oliver had undergone an uneventful exam from stem to stern, his indigestion was clearly attributable to a drug regimen that was easily adjusted, and his afternoon (except for the immobility) seemed about as reminiscent of the good old days as I could have imagined at this stage. At last, it felt acceptable to throttle back just a notch.

If there were ever a justification for the moniker *Miracle Man*, then the seventh day out of ICU was the time for pinning that badge on Oliver's lapel. Over the prior two nights, Ollie had resumed his normal pattern of blissful, uninterrupted dozing, not emerging from the family bed until about an hour after the rest of the clan had been summoned for its morning *lacka-walka* (dog-speak for "walk around the lake"). In just one week, Oliver had managed to find a plateau of tranquility that few of us could possibly aspire to after being paralyzed from the waist down, hooked up to IV tubes for ten days, and engaged in mortal combat with a life-threatening disease. But the peaceful slumber of the past two nights was not the miracle—that was just the magician's opening act. The miracle itself is best told in the journal entry that I penned at the end of that fateful seventh day:

> *Oliver had his follow-up exam today at high noon with his neurologist and emergency vet Dr. Julie Ducote. Normally a bit fidgety en route to any appointment, Oliver was the embodiment of Zen-like contentment. Our clan leader must have known how this movie would end.*
>
> *After having follow-up radiographs to check on the extent of the remaining pleural fluid that surrounded his lungs and the changes (if any) in the suspicious mass in his chest, Dr. Ducote and her colleague Dr. Hayashi walked in with the results: the pleural fluid caused by pyothorax was no*

longer detectable and, most astonishing of all, the mass that was thought to be malignant had totally disappeared from the X-rays. Dr. Ducote sent along the radiographs to the same outside oncology expert who had thought it to be cancer in the first place, with a note that simply read, "Where did it go?"

The suspicious mass was nowhere to be found—it had simply disappeared. Four different vets had examined the prior radiographs, and the impressive mass was clearly visible to all, having been described with those dreaded words "suspected carcinoma." Cancer is a resourceful and formidable enemy, and a malignant mass doesn't just disappear like that. What had it been? Where had it gone? It was anyone's guess. Only the Miracle Man knows for sure, and I couldn't care less. The only thing that mattered was that the mass wasn't inside our boy anymore.

Do you believe in miracles? Well, I will tell you this—I believe in the Miracle Man—and I now believe to a certainty that his promise of one hundred days will be fulfilled. My fingers are just dancing across the keyboard! Boy, is it ever a cake-walk to cherish today!

After the mysterious disappearance of the mass on Oliver's radiographs and the complete absence of pleural fluid around his lungs, I desperately needed time to allow the impact of that appointment to sink in. It was time to relish the progress of the past week. Our boy was well on his way to proving that his ICU rally was not a onetime fluke, that there was something truly incredible about this guy's ability to marshal his strength when it was needed most.

Later that evening when I was all alone in my study with a bottle of Corona gripped tightly in my hand, I reflected back on the day twenty-five years before when Dr. Steve Stephens, a radiologist at Dallas's Medical City, emerged from studying my own CT scan to deliver the verdict as to whether the impressive mass in my head was a malignant brain tumor. Six months earlier, when the lesion was first detected after a series of epileptic seizures, I had opted not to undergo surgery to remove it, in order to avoid the brain damage that might well result from the procedure itself. It was a risky decision, but it was mine alone—the neurology team was unanimously in favor of immediate surgical intervention in case the mass was malignant. But I was convinced that it was not or, more accurately, I decided to let the drama play out another six months. If it were malignant, I would have been in more desperate straits after allowing it to grow unchecked in that time; but if it were not, I would have dodged the bullet of slicing into my brain tissue to extract the offending lesion.

I wasn't able to pull off Oliver's Houdini-like disappearing act, but I was able to listen to the radiologist deliver his six-month verdict with a sense of personal vindication: "You were right all along—the mass is slightly smaller—and a malignant tumor would not shrink in that period of time." The ultimate verdict of "arteriovenous malformation" was still a cause for concern and potentially dangerous, but it wasn't a malignant brain tumor and it wasn't a death sentence. Like Oliver, I walked out of the radiologist's office with a new lease on life.

The few days that followed the miracle appointment with Dr. Ducote were reminiscent of days of yore. Oliver "held court" in the kitchen most of the day surrounded by his posse, ate his regular meals and retained the nourishment without incident, slept a good portion of the day, and underwent his three regular sessions of home rehab therapy.

I sometimes stared at Oliver and wondered whether his memory still retained images of chasing squirrels around the lake or standing paw-to-paw with Henry on those occasions long ago when Henry would mount a challenge to his authority. I asked myself whether Oliver thought of walking and trotting as skills that had simply deserted him—or whether instead there was no memory of that at all. I also wondered whether Oliver remembered when his eyesight was pin-sharp, or did our boy just assume that the blurry outline of shapes and objects was simply what everyone else saw.

I had no way of knowing, but my guess was that Oliver, like all great survivors, had the mental toughness and discipline to accept the cards that were dealt him, without regret or longing for a fresh set of cards. You could tell that Ollie was beginning to view his daily routines in a different light. It was as if the physical limitations that we might have found so depressing were for him no more than the circumstances that had ushered in a new phase in his life. What counted most for Oliver had never been the use of his limbs in feats of strength or daring but the presence of his clan and his loved ones around him—and that had not changed one whit.

We were watching our boy grow stronger by the day. It was good to return to normal in the sense that "normal" was most meaningful to him—but it was also good to remind ourselves not to take "normal" for granted ever again.

It's amazing in retrospect how the near miss of losing Oliver to pyothorax and the threat of cancer placed everything in perspective, particularly his lower leg paralysis—however temporary or permanent that would prove to be. Just ten days earlier, I was literally praying for a return home, and the paralysis barely entered my mind—and now that was exactly what we had. Oliver was at home and admittedly less mobile than before the accident—but his strength was returning, his attitude was great, and my occasional frustration with his inability to be more mobile was no more than a passing annoyance. Even the partial paralysis itself had spawned its own episodes of joy, such as the ninth day after ICU when I received a call from his therapist, Jennie, that his wheels had arrived from the manufacturer almost one week early and would be all set for a fitting at his upcoming rehab appointment.

Merriam-Webster defines *perspective* as "the aspect in which a subject or its parts are mentally viewed; esp: a view of things . . . in their true relationship or relative importance." The word *cherish* is not in there, but it might as well be. Viewed in its "true relationship or relative importance," our ability to cherish every day with Oliver on a journey that we expected to last at least one hundred days afforded quite a different perspective on those two rear legs.

Chapter Four

Burning Rubber

Days 10-13

I AM PROBABLY NOT THE MOST OBSERVANT member of the Jewish faith—but I am nevertheless a strong adherent to the fundamental tenets of Judaism. I am also a devout believer in omens and superstitions. Years ago, when I first began to travel to Africa on photo safaris, I clipped off a lock of hair from each of our four-legged guys and stuffed the clumps in an empty medicine vial. Before leaving on each trip, I would kiss the canister one time for each member of the clan as a form of invocation for their well-being during my absence—not exactly a time-honored tradition akin to the groom crushing the wine glass at the end of a Jewish marriage ceremony, but I never risked cutting my lip from kissing the plastic vial.

On Oliver's tenth day out of ICU, our family celebrated two major milestones that were somehow spiritually linked in my mind—Rosh Hashanah (the Jewish New Year) and

Oliver's first day of mobility in his brand-new "rear legs" thanks to the arrival of his customized set of wheels.

A Talmudic scholar might search the ancient scrolls in vain for a mystical connection between the first of the Ten High Holy Days and a hunk of metal tubing and rubber wheels that gave the Miracle Man a second chance at mobility. But I will never be convinced that there wasn't something intensely spiritual about Oliver's first day in his new chariot falling on the same date that Jews congregate the world over to celebrate the start of a fresh year.

In his morning rehab session, Jennie fitted Ollie into his customized scooter, hoping that he would be amongst those canines that take to their wheels right away and figure out how to work this newfangled contraption. Thankfully, even before Jennie had finished tightening the screws on the frame so that the rear wheels would be aligned with the exact contours of his body, Oliver was off to the races—wending his way around the therapy room—burning rubber! After a prolonged scream of "Yes Sirrrrrr!!!" I calmed down and began to wonder what might be going through the mind of this very pensive and intelligent creature—for weeks unable to take a single step on his own and then suddenly breezing along without any human hands at work.

His back legs were clearly passengers on this abbreviated road trip—just dangling there in the rear stirrups and delighted to be along for the ride. I could almost imagine him thinking: *Oh man, it feels so good to be tooling around on my own!*

By early afternoon, Oliver was moving around our property in his shiny new scooter, sniffing the grass and then deciding that the bushes offered more pungent odors to be savored. In the process of navigating through his most familiar haunts—in short spurts of only a few yards each— Ollie was restoring a sense of order to the homestead that had been sorely missed in the past couple of weeks. It was a touching scene to behold, and it had such a poignant note of normalcy to it—just a dog walking around in the backyard.

A few hours later, as sunset arrived to signal the start of the Jewish holiday, I was seated in Temple Emanu-El listening as the rabbi sounded the shofar to usher in the Hebrew New Year. I have little doubt that I was the only member of the congregation that day whose misty eyes reflected not only the sense of melancholy for loved ones who could no longer be amongst us and the gift of family members who could, but also the glorious thought that the head of our clan was in motion once again.

I am generally regarded as a hard-nosed negotiator in the investment field (a calling that may be thought of as the financial equivalent of mud wrestling), but I am a very emotional guy in my personal life—you just have to punch the right button and all the raw emotions that were suppressed decades ago escape in a gusher. Whenever I watch the final scene in the movie *Field of Dreams* in which Kevin Costner's character plays a game of catch with his long-estranged father, I am in serious need of a box of tissues. It is an eerie reminder of my favorite early childhood memory when Dad would come home after work, toss off his tie, grab the catcher's mitt, and go into a crouch to handle my blazing fastball. The scene that morning of Oliver immediately taking to his new set of wheels pushed the right button.

Over the next few days, Oliver basked in the glow of blissful mobility to the stunned silence of his mates. Obviously, the clan had never seen anything as bizarre as his scooter in their entire lives. Until the other guys had watched him being lifted in and out of his chariot over and over again, it is quite possible that the consensus among Ollie's posse was that their leader had somehow mysteriously sprouted a new set of round legs and some metal armor along his sides. The initial apprehension within the clan was reminiscent of the reason why safari-goers in the wilds of Africa are constantly admonished not to exit their jeep on a game drive—until you step out of the vehicle, predators seem to think that you are part and parcel of that fearsome, smoke-belching hunk of metal that resembles a squared-off rhino. Once you do step out, however, it becomes abundantly clear to the predator that you are just a two-legged animal that is fair game for an attack.

In no time at all, Ollie was trundling about the yard in multiple outdoor sessions each day, managing to handle the steering of his vehicle with great dexterity. In the fairly tall grass, soggy from seven straight days of rain, it was a bit of a struggle at first but Ollie powered through. Once back inside the kitchen, our boy pedaled around with only the occasional bounce against the center island.

In one of my more frivolous moments, I even had time to compose an e-mail from Oliver to his cousin Bosley, who had just moved into a new apartment in the Chelsea district of New York with our daughter Vanessa and her fiancé Gavin:

Hey Boz! How goes it, man? How are the new digs? I know from experience it can be rough when you have to adjust to a new place. I hear you went from the West Side to the East Side . . . fancy-schmancy! It may take a while for you to break in the new routes. I have a lot of rough-and-tumble friends in New York, so if you need a bit of protection in the new 'hood, let me know.

Things here are scorching! I have my new scooter, and I just love it! I actually trotted today with no leash on and no goddamn towel around my waist to do my business— that towel routine is so demeaning for a clan leader. All the other guys are a bit jealous that I'm the only one with wheels, but I earned this thing with my own blood, sweat, and tears.

Well, stay cool, man . . . can't wait to see you again in the Parrot [a tiny island in the Turks & Caicos]. By the way, Bobby decided

to name our place in Parrot Cay "Oliver's Cove" . . . pretty cool, huh? Well, as the saying goes, "Leadership has its privileges."
Love you, man!

> *Oliver Winston Haas,*
> *Clan Leader Extraordinaire*

In the days that followed, Oliver began to settle into a comfortable routine—leisurely naps in the kitchen with the clan, scooting derrière-style across its tiled floor when not in his wheels, frequent business breaks near the lake, and thrice-daily home therapy sessions. Incredibly, the strength and coordination in his back legs had progressed to the point that Ollie was able to stand unassisted on all fours for a few seconds before swaying at the stern end and gently returning to earth in the sitting position. It was an unmistakable sign that while his spinal cord had been severely damaged, there were still neural pathways in partial operation that could carry a signal from his brain to his rear limbs and urge him forth.

At peace with himself and ever the Professor, Oliver was conducting a tutorial for all those within his orbit on how to handle extreme adversity and accept challenges as the spicier ingredients of that recipe called life. Even months later, I am hard-pressed to decide whether Oliver viewed his wheels as the least bit inferior to two flesh-and-bone limbs. For a dog, this device certainly carries none of the emotional baggage that some people ascribe to the wheelchair-bound of the humanoid species. And for Oliver, the things that mattered most in his life—the human and canine members of his family—were definitely "wheelchair accessible."

Buoyed by the miracle of Oliver's emergence from ICU and his becoming mobile once again—all within the span of less than two weeks—I thought incessantly about his plucky spirit and reveled in his many accomplishments. Though equally impressed with his progress, on occasion Candice grew melancholy and needed a nudge to take a look at how far we had traveled since his fateful tumble and those fragile days in intensive care. I didn't think of Oliver as fragile . . . but I had always thought of life as fragile. We must all absorb blindside hits in the unscripted journey that unfolds one day at a time; how we absorb those hits is what ultimately determines where that journey will lead.

On the thirteenth day after ICU, Ollie and I initiated a new tradition—a beer together on the porch just outside my study after my return home at the end of a long day that often began at 4:00 a.m. On the inaugural day of this new tradition, we were inundated by swarms of mosquitoes that had temporarily taken over our rain-soaked property, so we bid a hasty retreat into the study. Hunkered down in one of my stuffed armchairs, I sipped a Corona and lime with my boy on my lap. Knocking down a brew or two at the end of the day with your best friend is one of the greatest traditions ever invented.

Chapter Five

Crisis in the Ranks

Days 14-16

AS EACH SUCCEEDING DAY MARKED ANOTHER mini-stride forward for the Miracle Man, we encountered a vivid reminder that Oliver was not the only vulnerable member of a clan that had grown a bit long in the tooth. We learned from a veterinary gastro specialist what had caused Elmer's two days of periodic vomiting: Ollie's first lieutenant had apparently swallowed a large foreign object that would cause serious internal bleeding if not removed immediately—either via a simple extraction through his throat or, if that proved unsuccessful, through major abdominal surgery.

In what would become a two-ring circus of shuttling back and forth between the two, Elmer's drama unfolded in the same clinic—and at almost precisely the same time of day—as Ollie's weekly rehab session. To say the least, I had my hands full with the clan's two eldest statesmen. The slight difference in their respective timetables allowed Oliver to be dropped off at rehab just before Elmer was scheduled to head upstairs for his throat extraction (or endoscopy). While waiting with Elmer for Oliver's session to begin in the slick, polished hallway outside of rehab—an ideal surface for Ollie to spin his wheels—the clan leader was as frisky as could be. Oliver chased his buddy Elmer up and down the hallway at breakneck speed to the delight of any passersby. It was an apt metaphor for my own frantic movements in the two days that lay ahead.

In a very positive sign of neurological progress, while in hot pursuit of Elmer, Ollie was wagging his tail from side to side at a furious pace—as opposed to the more deliberate up-and-down movement that we had seen ever since his accident. In the rehab session itself, Ollie showed a bit of back hip movement for the first time, another indication that those neural pathways were allowing some traffic through from brain to limb.

For his part, Elmer soon became the focus of attention as his internist Dr. Rifkin readied him for his endoscopy, while a surgical team was poised across the hallway for the more invasive abdominal procedure in the event that Dr. Rifkin's fishing expedition through his throat proved unsuccessful. Given my fervent belief in omens, I was delighted to see from her diplomas that Dr. Rikfin had completed her residency at the *Elmer* and Mamdouha Bobst Hospital.

Once I left Elmer in Dr. Rifkin's care for his afternoon procedure, I headed home with Oliver to await the results of the endoscopy. The drive back with only Ollie beside me was a downer emotionally. Given that my insides were still raw from the ICU ordeal, leaving a clan member behind in a vet clinic felt much more ominous than it turned out to be.

After a few hours of hand-wringing, I received a call in the early evening from Dr. Rifkin reporting that she had successfully extracted three sizeable chunks of jagged black plastic without the need for any surgery. Nicknamed "Perfect Boy" ever since his graduation *phi barka kappa* from obedience school, Elmer had performed just perfectly. Still groggy and with a subnormal temperature from the anesthesia, Elmer spent the night at the clinic, where coincidentally I had an appointment later the next morning with another member of the clan. Within a few hours of Elmer's waking up on the day after surgery, I would be chaperoning brother Henry to a follow-up visit with his orthopedist to gauge how well steroids had fought off the immune-mediated arthritis that had laid him low a few weeks before. The Over-the-Hill Gang was still hanging in there, but the march of Father Time was leaving a few footprints along the landscape of their medical charts.

Later that night, when Ollie and I reprised our tradition of a beer at the end of the day, I let out a deep breath and moaned, "Shit man, I need a break—this fire drill stuff at the clinic is beating me to a pulp!" Oliver just looked up at me and licked the perspiring sides of the Corona bottle.

For once, the Miracle Man was not the first case in the triage hierarchy of the clan. Elmer's release from overnight recovery following his "scope" to remove the slices of plastic had to rank as "top gun" in the infirmary wing. Upon his return, a still woozy Elmer snoozed almost the entire day on one of the many pillow beds in the kitchen.

Henry (himself ten years old) had done equally well at the appointment with his orthopedist. Dr. Radasch confirmed that the blast of steroids given him to combat his sudden onset of arthritis placed him squarely within the majority of cases that do recover from this excruciating condition, in which the immune system inexplicably attacks the joints, literally bringing its host to his knees. When both Elmer and Henry returned from the clinic, Oliver for once was among the clan greeters instead of being at the opposite end of the ritual. For my part, I was wondering whether I had a legitimate claim for asking the clinic to name a wing after the Haas family for its unflinching and outrageously expensive support of the practices of three different vet groups in the span of just two calendar days—if not a wing, then at least an operating room.

Meanwhile, in the midst of all the zaniness of my attending to his clan comrades, Oliver's ambulatory progress—both in rehab and at home—continued in small steps. Ollie was just beginning to rotate his back hips ever so slightly whenever his front legs moved forward in his scooter, clearly imitating the traditional four-step motion. We measured his advances in smaller increments, but all was moving in the right direction. Our distance from the brink continued to increase with each passing day.

On the sixteenth day post-ICU, my office offered no refuge from the trauma of the past few days—nothing critical, just the cumulative effect of an impending deadline for the latest project with Nat Geo, a few employee-related issues that demanded immediate attention, and a heightened level of activity in the investment portfolio.

By the end of the day, my nerves were shot. Once I arrived home, I dropped my briefcase just inside the door, released the hounds on a prolonged *lacka-walka,* and proceeded to strap Ollie into his scooter for his mellower version of a walk around the lake. All I did after that was stroll beside the Miracle Man.

Ollie didn't do anything particularly dramatic on that walk—a few spins and one or two lively trots. But he did do something impactful and infectious. Our boy sniffed the air repeatedly, taking in all the scents that a canine's incredible nose can inhale, advanced a few steps at a time, and casually looked around with eyes that had almost succumbed to advanced cataracts. After fifteen minutes or so, Ollie tilted his head my way to assure himself that I was still right beside him. It was only then that I calmed down—this old fellow in his chariot with virtually no eyesight managed to remind me through those milky eyes, "Hey man, life is good—lean back and enjoy it while it lasts."

Just like any best friend, Oliver instinctively knew how to comfort me. By the end of our stroll around the lake, all the tension had left my body, the minor irritations of the day had evaporated, and we walked back home together.

Chapter Six

Coyote Standoff

Days 17-19

FOR THE FIRST TIME SINCE OLIVER'S ACCIDENT almost one month before, we returned to our Malibu mountainside retreat—the proverbial scene of the crime, where Ollie had suffered his fall. I definitely had trepidations about the prospect of seeing that embankment where he had taken a tumble. But our boy did not display the slightest sign of aversion at all. As soon as we walked through the front door, Ollie put on a marvelous display of wheel-maneuvering, barking, and playful antics—no bad memories of the place whatsoever.

Memory is a strange thing. As with many of the most potent forces in life—money, technology, and power—memory is decidedly a two-edged sword. It is at the core of love and tradition and even survival . . . but it is also the seat of nightmares and resentment and anxiety. It is fascinating how animals, both in the wild and in the home, seem to filter out the more disabling side of memory in favor of the powerful role it plays in preserving life. Elephants and other migrating herds have an uncanny ability to retrace pathways to fertile lands that have been followed for generations, while mother cheetahs seem to have an equally impressive ability to jettison any recollection of cubs that have perished, in favor of moving on with the business of life. Domesticated canines seem to recall the scent of people who have been met only once or twice before, but also manage to bypass the anxiety that might otherwise infect a place such as our California home that had been the scene of a crippling injury.

Ollie scooted around the house at will, as the mountain winds carried through the screen door a fresh dose of news from the critters that roam free in the park surrounding our home. Apparently, he harbored no fears and no bad memories.

After I was able to pinpoint the most logical flat surface for a long walk, Ollie and I exited the gate by our home at the foothills of the Santa Monica Mountains and marched proudly down the pathway. The street surface was relatively smooth as were the adjacent grass and dirt paths. Ollie strolled along in his truck all the way down the full length of the lane until it looped around in a graceful cul-de-sac.

When we reached the end, we turned around and started the long trek back. As we moved closer to home, I was able to spot Candice right in front of our gate, screaming and waving her arms furiously back and forth. At first, I thought this might be an enthusiastic greeting for our two-wheeled hiker, but then it dawned on me that such histrionics would be totally out of character for the normally reserved Candice.

As we got closer, I noticed that she was armed with a large broom and was shouting something about carrying Ollie and his scooter back, pointing toward the mountain that overlooked the front of our property. As we headed nonchalantly along the pathway toward our front gate, we discovered the cause for Candice's alarm. A group of five large coyotes were clearly visible in the foothills, closer to our property than we had ever seen during daylight hours. It was not at all unusual to discover the nocturnal droppings of coyotes in the morning when we woke up or to be serenaded by their howling in the middle of the night. Our property is almost totally surrounded by California State Park, and that land belongs to whomever and whatever chooses to roam free within its borders. But a pack of coyotes this close to the edge of our property in broad daylight was something else.

As we headed back toward our gate at a deliberate pace, the individual members of the coyote troop became more and more distinct to the naked eye. Every single one was frozen still, and the largest of the group (presumably *their* clan leader) was quite impressive in size, considerably larger than any of the ones I had ever spotted before. We were clearly the object of their concentration.

Our own clan leader had probably detected the presence of the strangers when we were further up the road, as his pinpoint sense of smell (the one sense that had not yet begun to desert him) surely noticed the intrusion. As we approached our front gate, his stiffened neck and upraised nose left no doubt that Oliver was on alert and aware of the presence of the coyote pack. But we were not about to be intimidated in front of our own property, nor was it a particularly good idea to make a mad dash for our gate and thereby imitate prey animals that would instinctively flee coyote predators. Instead we continued moving along at our own confident pace. With the foothills to our right and the gate straight ahead, we closed the gap to our property under the watchful gaze of this other clan. My experience in the African bush came in handy that day; having been charged on different occasions by lions, hippos, crocs, and elephants, I had faced hostile critters before and lived to tell about my misadventures. And for his part, the big guy—who had overcome pyothorax and immune-mediated attacks on his life—was not about to cower before a mere pack of coyotes threatening to become trespassers on the turf that was his solemn duty to protect. I had never once seen Oliver back down from a scrape with other creatures—no matter how large or how many—and this was not about to be the first time.

The Miracle Man trundled all the way back to our front gate at a defiant pace with an air of *c'est la vie* in his gait. As I punched in the security code that would open the automated gates and permit access to our property, Ollie turned and lifted his head, sniffed the air one last time, and reminded the still-frozen coyotes that their right to wander the surrounding hills ended at our front gate.

For good measure, on the day after this standoff, Ollie and I undertook a trio of scooter walks down the very same lane, retracing the steps where his now legendary coyote encounter had taken place. On our first walk, there were no coyotes in sight, but Oliver's stroll did arouse the ire and ferocious barking of the security dog that polices our closest neighbor's home. We were about twenty feet away from the iron fencing that surrounds his property when the "bark-bark-bark" exchange broke out between Oliver and his counterpart next door.

Ollie decided that twenty feet was too great a distance for him to express the full extent of his wrath at being disturbed by a hound at least three times his size, so our boy ran in his chariot up to the fence to make sure that his retorts could be heard loud and clear. The scooter-assisted running was indeed a brand-new milestone for the Miracle Man—hardly an easy gear to access when you're harnessed into a two-wheeled contraption. After making his point, Oliver sauntered away toward home.

Our final day in Malibu was devoid of any standoffs or near fisticuffs, just a time to savor the mountain breezes and the events of the past few weeks. Despite all his disabilities in the traditional sense of the word, Ollie had figured out how to squeeze as many drops of nectar as possible out of a long and eventful life-arc, how to extend the dignity of life when it is approaching its sunset, and how to gather those two-leggers who love you and those four-leggers who respect you into an ever-tightening circle that seemed to keep the literal and proverbial coyotes at bay.

Chapter Seven

Practicing Our Good-byes

Days 20-23

THE MIRACLE MAN TRIUMPHANTLY RETURNED from his California tour of duty, and the following morning I departed for a three-day business trip, my first since his release from ICU. I had absolutely no concerns that Ollie would be well attended in my absence, but it was a strange feeling nevertheless. We all tend to entertain misgivings about leaving loved ones in the aftermath of a health crisis, and this was certainly no exception.

Bereft of Oliver's company, I briefly recalled a considerably more agonizing separation from him almost eight years before when his life was at risk, and we had no choice but to leave him behind as Candice and I headed off to the 2002 World Cup in Leipzig, Germany, to watch our daughter, Vanessa, compete in the equestrian championships.

That cycle of events was triggered in the midst of a design session with my New York publishing firm, when I had been interrupted by an urgent call from my assistant, Christine, back in Dallas. Over the years, the term *urgent* had been applied to a wide range of subjects that required immediate attention—securities trades that had to be acted on in a matter of minutes, unanticipated breakdowns in negotiations, wire transfers that had gone AWOL within the labyrinth of the banking system. But there was only one category that actually deserved that label—a health crisis. Unfortunately, this interruption was truly urgent.

In a tone that I had learned to associate with particularly bad news, Christine explained that Oliver was in serious danger from a rare blood disorder. In the course of a routine dental procedure, Oliver's gums began to bleed heavily, and the vet discovered a host of dark red splotches all along his belly and chest. The spots were clearly the result of capillary bleeding just below the surface of his skin. The dental procedure was cut short, and emergency blood tests revealed that Oliver was suffering from a rare and unpronounceable blood condition known as immune-mediated thrombocytopenia. In the alphabet soup of medical jargon, IMT is a seldom seen but potentially deadly disorder in which the body's own immune system actually destroys a major clotting agent in the bloodstream known as platelets (a word that we would become all too familiar with in the weeks ahead). With the platelet level reduced dramatically, the blood effectively becomes so watery thin that the body becomes vulnerable to either spontaneous hemorrhaging (hence the red spots on Oliver's abdomen where tiny capillaries had allowed blood to seep out) or excessive bleeding from any internal or external trauma.

On the bright side (and there were not a whole bunch of bright spots to choose from), Oliver was in no discomfort whatsoever. From a clinical point of view, our boy was oblivious to the war being waged inside his body as the immune system sensed some imagined foreign agent within the blood and systematically attacked his platelets in an effort to rid the body of this supposed intruder. In the process, the blood had lost its natural capacity to clot, and the risk of a deadly hemorrhage from an internal organ (including the brain) was ever-present. It was difficult to escape the analogy of a walking time bomb with a wagging tail.

In the weeks ahead, Oliver would be administered an increasingly potent barrage of steroids in an effort to suppress the immune system and turn the tide against the relentless internal attack upon its host. Every few days, we would await the results of his blood tests for evidence that the drugs were taking hold in their effort to restore the platelet count to its normal range of 160-200. But we were destined to embark on an emotionally draining roller-coaster ride as his platelet count rallied back from 30 to 75, only to sink as low as 3 and then recover to 121 before falling precipitously once again, this time below 10.

Frustrated in our attempts to stabilize Oliver, we brought in a specialist who had often treated this disorder over the years and whose philosophy meshed with our own: intervene as aggressively as possible with extremely heavy doses of steroids until the body responds by suppressing the immune system from wreaking its havoc. There were dangers galore from artificially shutting down the body's natural defense system, but we concurred that there was simply no other choice at this point.

Oliver endured a fresh battery of tests in order to eliminate the nastiest explanations for his brand of IMT—such as a cancerous mass. When the results came back, we took refuge in the news that the most fearsome of causes had been banished from the field of play. We were left with the medical profession's timeworn label *idiopathic*—meaning that we don't have the foggiest idea what's causing this condition.

In an effort to stave off any possible bruising that can cause excessive bleeding, we were forced to separate Ollie from his clan for fear of injury from the wrestling that is part and parcel of clan life. Only Elmer, the gentle second eldest member, was permitted to keep him company. The steroids caused Oliver to suffer from an unquenchable thirst and a rapacious appetite. Allowed free access to water, the ever-dignified clan leader was humiliated by his occasional accidents.

We all did our best to learn how to live with Oliver's condition. Without a clear clan leader, the other four canines (Cooper was not aboard yet) resembled a nursery school class with a substitute teacher—all disorganized play with no clear lines of authority. Even Henry, who normally coveted the throne that Oliver ascended each day, seemed disoriented without Ollie's heavy-pawed discipline. We were afforded a glimpse ahead to the day when the clan would need to fend for itself without its original alpha male.

Candice was inconsolable and her usual plucky attitude evaporated in a wave of pessimism. In the face of a health crisis, human or canine, Candice normally rouses the troops à la Joan of Arc, but the onset of this crisis had been so sudden and so inscrutable that she withdrew into herself, fearing the worst at any moment. I encouraged her to act normally around Oliver, who was exceptionally bright and attuned to our moods. I was convinced that the immune system was as linked to one's mental attitude as any part of the body, and Oliver had to be insulated from the contagion of pessimism.

For my part, I never believed for one moment, not even when his platelet count descended into single digits, that we would lose Oliver. In the course of his treatment, I was struck by the similarities between Oliver's condition and my own health crises of years past. I too had suffered through periods in which either a neurological or cardiac disorder could have had disastrous consequences at any moment—the "walking time bomb" syndrome.

Banished into virtual isolation from his clan, Ollie took long walks with me around the lake by our home. Our pace was measured, and we were transported back to the days when Ollie's clan consisted only of humans. I was impressed by the inherent dignity of this creature and his ability to connect with his master on an emotional and spiritual level. It was in the course of these long walks each day that I became utterly convinced that this blood disorder would not be Oliver's undoing. Instead, it was destined to be a stage in his life, and I was there to comfort him, just as he had comforted me over the years when our roles had been reversed.

It was in the midst of this crisis that Candice and I had to leave for a one-week trip to Germany. Vanessa was about to participate in the 2002 Equestrian World Cup Championships in Leipzig as one of the youngest competitors, male or female, from any nation. In more normal circumstances, this would have been a joyous interlude, capping fourteen years of blood, sweat, and tears devoted to Vanessa's riding career.

But we still had to say good-bye to Oliver before we left. I took him into my bathroom and snipped off a lock of his hair, placing it in the empty medicine vial that would accompany me everywhere I went from then on, from the canyons of Wall Street to the savanna grasslands of Africa. I cupped Oliver's head between my two hands and explained in a firm voice that we would be away for one week, only about half as long as my regular safaris to Africa several times each year. I calmly assured him that this blood condition would ultimately be banished from his body, his rightful place as clan leader would be restored, and life would go on as before. We kissed good-bye, as I planted several smooches squarely on his thin, black lips, and Oliver doused me with a series of saliva-heavy licks from his pink tongue. I refused to allow my mood to convey any sense of foreboding, and the fact is that I felt quite confident that Ollie would overcome this crisis. All we were doing was practicing our good-byes so that when the ultimate good-bye arrived at some point in the future, we would be ready.

One week later, after having scrolled through daily faxes from the vet that relayed Ollie's test results, we left Leipzig and returned to a clan leader who was clearly on the mend. The crisis had passed—and there was no further need to practice our good-byes.

In contrast with the melancholy of that flashback, upon my return to Dallas on Day 22, I was greeted not only by a cluster of wagging tails and licking tongues but also by a double-barreled barrage of good news on the vet and rehab fronts. On the vet side, I accompanied Oliver on his triumphant return to the emergency clinic that had housed his ICU saga weeks before, this time for a post-discharge evaluation by Dr. Ducote. The Miracle Man strutted through the clinic door to a standing ovation from the staff, which saw him for the first time in the new wheels that had become a regular fixture of his daily life. Ollie proceeded to explore virtually every examining room completely on his own to the delight of the crowd that had gathered around. Before his actual exam, Oliver fertilized the waiting room sufficiently that I would not have been surprised to see palm trees thriving there on our next visit.

Shortly afterward, Drs. Ducote and Hayashi whisked him away to check on whether there was any excess fluid around his lungs and confirm that the suspicious mass in his chest had not returned. During that brief hiatus when I sat alone in a wooden chair in the exam room, my supreme confidence in Ollie's recovery suffered a blow to the midsection. While I had no reason to suspect a backward slide, I literally sat on my hands until the vets returned. But the Miracle Man never seemed to be in doubt as to what the verdict would be—lungs as clean as a newborn puppy. Well, perhaps that's a bit of an exaggeration—but "clear as a bell" was indeed the verdict rendered by Dr. Ducote.

At his next rehab session, Ollie continued to display more of the rear hip movement that is often the first sign of at least partial recovery from paralysis. It's strange how I greeted the news that he might be gaining more use of his back legs— obviously that was a thrilling prospect, but I didn't want to be greedy and set another tall obstacle in front of him. We had been exceedingly blessed with the mobility and strength that Ollie had already achieved and the near perfect repair to the shattered pieces of his life. I felt it would be good to bear in mind that the promise I had extracted from Oliver in ICU was simply *one hundred days*—that we would be granted at least one hundred more days in each other's company—and after all, a deal is a deal.

Chapter Eight

Just a Hunk of Metal

Days 24-28

IN THE BRIEF SPAN OF ONLY FIVE DAYS, THE CLAN celebrated two momentous occasions, one of deeply religious significance and the other a decidedly more secular event— and in the midst of the festivities, I would pay homage to a pair of contraptions that played a pivotal role in Oliver's recovery.

Each day in this one-hundred-day saga started and ended with its own routine. I am admittedly a creature of habit, and if I am jolted off track, I can easily descend into a bit of a funk. I usually wake up well before 5:00 a.m., brew my coffee, head down to my study, log onto the computer, and sip that java as I prep for the day. I need that time alone in utmost quiet, knowing that all is well with Candice and the guys in the bedroom directly above my head. Actually it's just the five boys that sleep in our bed—for reasons of modesty

I suppose, sister Chloe always sleeps in the laundry room downstairs. This routine is my compass, my gyroscope for achieving balance each day. I savor not only the coffee and the rush that the caffeine instills near the end of that first cup, but also the grounding and perspective that this private time lends to the day ahead.

In a very real sense, the predawn belongs to me. The last few hours before sunrise are my most effective, most creative, and most peaceful time of day. It is within this slot that for several weeks after each photo shoot, I study the details of five thousand to ten thousand images, searching for the handful that will find their way into a published work. It is inside this cocoon where I meticulously plot each thrust and parry in the duel of a pending negotiation. It is during this exceedingly personal time that I retreat into whatever realm my Zen-induced meditation chooses for its destination. In brief, it is within this predawn netherworld when I am at my best—undistracted, uninterrupted, and wholly unwitnessed. If I were an athlete at this hour, I'd be swatting home runs inside an empty stadium, in front of a crowd made up exclusively of ushers and hot dog vendors. It is how I hoard three or four hours each day, squirreling away the time needed to support two radically different lifestyles as an investor and a photographer-author. These early morning hours are the lubricant that allows an almost seamless transition between my personal version of Dr. Jekyll and Mr. Hyde, without either character becoming an unbearable monster.

After a few hours in my study, I head upstairs and bring the boys down in three separate shifts—first the Elmer-Spencer-Cooper brigade (who require no assistance in flying downstairs), then Henry, who needs to be carried to avoid the pounding on his chronically sore knees that the trek down the stairs entails, and finally our clan leader, who prefers a few minutes (or even an hour or so) of extra snooze time.

Once Ollie has logged a few more ZZZZs, it is time for his morning walk, which has developed its own ritual of sorts. After first relieving himself of urgent business demands, Oliver has the endearing habit of walking a few steps and sniffing the air in all directions—then repeating the same maneuver several times over. It's the canine equivalent of reading the morning paper—taking in all the news of the comings and goings of the night before. In the morning, I don't rush the big guy but simply allow him to browse the news at his leisure.

At the other end of the day, the evening routine of "last call before closing" is more of the same, only briefer. The final walk of the day is normally Candice's tour of duty, but for whatever reason, I manned that shift one night during his fourth week out of ICU. Oliver caught me off guard with an unanticipated burst of trotting toward the back gate when I had only a pair of white socks on to cushion my feet against the gravel drive. Since the driveway is relatively flat, his wheels could spin with virtually no resistance. We were flying; I was just about jogging to keep up with him. We reached the back gate, and I expected a slow, deliberate walk back to the house. I even bent down and inspected Oliver's chest to detect any signs that his breathing was labored after this unexpected sprint. But no, not stressed in the least. After a few more seconds of inquisitive sniffing, Ollie broke into a trot on the way home and kept up the pace almost all the way to the front door. When we started this one-hundred-day journey together, we vowed to cherish every single day. On this particular night, Ollie decided to extend his newfound vigor to the very end of the day, delivering a message that "cherishing today" meant the entire day.

While each day is special, some are more special than others. Day 24 was officially *bark mitz-paw* day (the canine equivalent of "bar mitzvah"), since it was Elmer's thirteenth birthday. This date is both a solemn and a festive milestone in the Jewish faith, as it traditionally marks the day on which a boy becomes a man, with all the attendant responsibilities that come to rest squarely on the young man's shoulders.

Thirteen years is only a small fraction of the life expectancy of a humanoid, whereas at a multiple of seven, it marks the passage of ninety-one years for a canine. The occasion for a four-legger and his family is a vivid reminder that there is cause for celebration if the bark mitz-paw boy is still alive. Last year, we celebrated Ollie's entry into Hebraic manhood with a service in the big master bed with the entire clan in attendance. Oliver wore a specially designed, small blue yarmulke with a six-pointed Hebrew star, while

Candice and I improvised a religious service that was just as abbreviated as it was disorganized.

As with Oliver the year before, we honored that sacred tradition this year for Elmer with the entire canine congregation assembled in the master bedroom. Elmer had been granted a special dispensation by the rabbi to skip his part of the Torah reading during the ceremony. He simply hadn't had the time or the emotional strength to devote to his rigorous bark mitz-paw studies in light of the trauma surrounding Oliver.

Nevertheless, it was a time to reflect on Elmer's thirteen years in our home as the first member of Ollie's clan. In hindsight, Elmer was probably the product of one of those dreaded puppy mills. At three months of age, with his adorable square face pressed up against the glass crate in the pet store, we fell in love with him right before Christmas 1996 but were unsure we could handle two young pups, as Oliver was barely one year old—amusing in retrospect, given that we eventually migrated up to six canines. I tried to persuade Candice to double the size of the clan, and we finally compromised by agreeing that we would adopt Elmer if the as-yet-unnamed puppy were still in the pet store on the day after Christmas.

Sure enough, on December 26, this jet black yorkie-poo was just sitting there in his crate with downcast eyes that pleaded for a more expansive home than the cramped confines of his glass cubicle. We rescued him immediately and spirited my second son off to his new digs. From the moment he met Oliver, Elmer was smitten with his older brother, who then gracefully assumed the mantle of clan leadership. Over the years, the addition of four other clan members, although a constant source of companionship and childish antics for Elmer, did nothing at all to dull his fervent love of Oliver.

In every sense of the word, Elmer blossomed into the canine version of a true *mensch* (in Yiddish, "a person of integrity and honor"). In his entire life, Elmer never met a person or a dog that was greeted with anything other than a furiously wagging tail and instant affection. Elmer saw no need to bark or growl—his world was not an evil place at all.

Soon after the yarmulke came off, it was time for a double-barreled birthday bash for Elmer and Spencer (who had just turned nine), complete with a singing balloon (when you pressed it, it yodeled), party hats, presents galore, and doggie cake and ice cream. I adhered to my superstitious habit of wolfing down a small piece of the canine birthday cake to Candice's utter disgust. Although I was never sure which store this culinary delicacy originated from, I always found it to be quite edible with a taste that remotely resembled human food.

In the midst of a week packed with religious and secular events marking canine birthdays, I was emotionally moved by two pieces of equipment that had been the focal point of Oliver's recovery—his wheels and his hydrotherapy tank. On Sunday afternoon, I lounged around with the guys and casually followed the action as the Dallas Cowboys lost another one in the final minute. What did capture my attention, however, was the sight of Oliver's chariot lying on its side in the kitchen. When I stared at that contraption, the emotion that I felt was actually one of fondness—fondness for his wheels. I thought about the sensation of being able to hoist Oliver into his vehicle and fasten him securely in place so that he could maneuver around the house and scoot all over our property. Even though I suffer from a nearly obsessive attraction to foreign sports cars, it was the first time in my life that I felt an emotional attachment to a hunk of metal. But the wheels actually gave him something that all the finest vets and the most potent prescriptions could not—mobility and self-esteem and parity with the other members of his clan.

A few days later, I felt inspired by what took place inside a different piece of equipment—a large, sophisticated tub of water. Technically speaking, it's a hydrotherapy tank, and it was to become the mainstay of Oliver's rehab sessions. In hydrotherapy, animals are hoisted into a see-through Plexiglas tank that then fills with water until it is up to their shoulders. Once inside, the patients are supported by a harness system, which is adjusted to their height, and a flotation device, which keeps their head above water. After the harness is in place and the tank is filled to shoulder height, a rubber treadmill at the bottom of the tank is switched on, and the patient is left with no choice but to march along to avoid sliding to the back of the enclosure. The hydro tank is an ingenious piece of equipment that offers partially paralyzed animals like Oliver the ability to begin to use their injured limbs in an enclosure where the strain of supporting the body's natural weight is greatly alleviated by the buoyancy of the water.

After Oliver was hoisted into the tank and the treadmill was engaged, he lifted his front legs up rather smartly, doing a respectable imitation of the Budweiser Clydesdales, all the while shuffling his back legs a bit to keep in sync with the front. Although he had performed this exercise routine once before, this was the first time I had seen Oliver in the tank, and I was impressed with how vigorous his movements were. His therapist, Jennie, set the treadmill timer at a full ten minutes, up two minutes from the last session. When Ollie tired noticeably in the eighth minute, I moved to the front of the tank, reached over the edge, and placed my hand directly against his nose, exhorting him to continue until the full regimen was completed. Even though clearly straining toward the end, Oliver met the challenge.

When Ollie emerged from the tank and was toweled off, I thought exhaustion would overtake him—but as soon as we were out in the hallway on our way to the parking lot, he was as frisky as ever. The chance to impress everyone with his prowess in that tub of water and the accolades that were showered upon him at the end of the session—not to mention the dog treats—were apparently all that was needed to revive him.

Over the course of the next few months, the hydro tank would develop into the main vehicle for building up Oliver's front leg strength and the stamina that allowed him to move around in his chariot, as well as the stimulus for the back end movement that would prove central to his partial recovery from paralysis.

With all the medical wizardry and sophistication at our disposal, it was actually two mechanical contraptions—a two-wheeled chariot on dry land and a hydro tank filled with water—that allowed Oliver to regain a level of vitality and mobility that was nothing short of inspiring.

Chapter Nine

Oliver – Zen Master

Days 29-32

GRACE UNDER PRESSURE—THAT'S A QUALITY I
hold in the highest regard—in my business dealings, in my
photographic work, and in my lectures. On Day 30, I gave a
speech to more than 350 children and on Day 31 another one
to almost 500 adults. I had been working on those speeches
for months, and I knew that being able to deliver each one
with grace would augment the impact of the presentations
immeasurably.

I learned long ago from my years as a competitive
swimmer that the key to maintaining grace under pressure
is preparation—the longer and the more intensive your
preparation, the greater your confidence as you approach
D-Day for your performance. You practice incessantly and
repeatedly imagine yourself barely out-touching a competitor
at the end of the race or delivering a moving lecture—you
imprint that image of success in your mind, and then the

actual race or lecture is simply the next in a series of identical events.

In the aftermath of Oliver's accident, I was sometimes left to wonder what could possibly have prepared him to endure the physical pressure that had imploded on his life—two successive bouts with a misdirected immune system, the gradual loss of virtually all his sight and hearing, and then his partial paralysis. And yet there stood Oliver, without the essential accoutrements of his inheritance as a great wolf (mobility, sight, hearing, teeth), demonstrating the most amazing grace under pressure. With his dignity and intellect totally intact and his incredible adaptability, Oliver had held fast to his position of clan hegemony and emerged every bit as content as I had ever seen him. Despite all the challenges that had come his way, I don't recall him ever being depressed.

When I stopped to think about it—and I often did during those one hundred days—the fourteen-year-old canine at my feet was teaching me a thing or two about what lay ahead in my later years. Once I grudgingly abandoned the notion that I might live forever, I knew it would take a great deal of preparation to handle my own decline with grace. If, in fact, grace under pressure is the result of intensive preparation, it's not very easy to prepare for advanced aging, something you don't wish to face or don't believe will ever happen to you. Undoubtedly one of Ollie's many splendid gifts has been helping me prepare for my own inevitable decline—I have been watching him carefully absorb the body blows of physical decline without any of those blows landing on the core of his dignity, his happiness, or his intellect. What a remarkable professor—a masterful teacher of a course we don't ever wish to enroll in.

And Oliver has taught me even more—the Professor was offering a tutorial in how to lose a loved one. The death of a family dog is often so utterly painful and disorienting. Adopting a puppy echoes the pattern of having a baby in one important respect—it is a conscious decision to bring into the family an adorable, totally dependent infant that you fall in love with from the first moment. Then follows a period of growth and training and companionship, and finally the bonds of love have wrapped themselves ever so tightly around the two of you.

I suspect that most humans in this chain of love and dependency with a puppy rarely give thought in the first few years to the prospect of that puppy's eventual death. And then suddenly the disparity in how we age has vaulted a nine-year-old dog to the point where it is actually older than a fifty-nine-year-old man. It is about then, or within another year or so, that the cruel trick that was embedded in our respective DNA in the first place begins to show its dreaded face—at that point, we have no choice but to face the reality that our dog most likely will die before we do. The canine-child that we took on its first walk to the lake and potty-trained on old newspapers has become arthritic and incontinent before our very eyes. The realization of our impending loss descends like a curtain that comes down at the end of the first act of a five-act play with a sign that says, "Show's over!"

By rallying so many times from the brink, Oliver has afforded extra time, over and over again, to escape for the moment from the grip of this twist of fate. The extra time has allowed me to accept the fact that this sequencing was actually part of the bargain that we struck in the first place. It has afforded time to talk to Oliver about his courage and the gifts that this guy has bestowed upon me for well over a decade. It has afforded time to memorialize my feelings for him and to gain the insight that his life has provided about my own. It has afforded the chance to look differently upon his clan mates who must inevitably follow the trail that Ollie is blazing with such class and dignity.

It was in the midst of this one-hundred-day journey with Oliver that the meditation practice I began roughly six months earlier paid some of its most handsome dividends. As I walked Oliver around in his chariot at the end of his first month out of ICU, the bizarre notion occurred to me that Ollie possessed all the essential traits of a true Zen Master. There seemed to be no obvious reason why a Zen Buddhist must be a two-legged creature. *Webster's New World College Dictionary* makes no reference at all to the number of legs that a Zen adherent must have to qualify: "*Zen* n. 1. a variety of Buddhism, now practiced esp. in Japan, Vietnam, and Korea, seeking to attain an intuitive illumination of mind and spirit through meditation. . . . 2. the teachings and discipline of this kind of Buddhism."

The only requirements seem to be the possession of "mind" and "spirit" through which one may attain intuitive enlightenment. Having spent more than fifteen years photographing animals in the wild and having shared my home with an ever-expanding clan of canines, I entertain no doubt whatsoever that our four-legged brethren possess minds whose powers and channels of sensory input are in many ways the equal of man's (and in other ways, clearly superior) and whose spirit is not bounded by many of the flaws that allow humans to shed blood out of revenge or for sport.

Oliver seems to have emerged over the past few months and years as a shining example of the essence of Zen Buddhism, possessing all the essential traits of a true Zen Master: *acute sensory perception*—failing sight and hearing have not diminished his ability to appreciate the raw beauty of the world around him; *mindfulness*—Oliver does indeed live in the present moment, unperturbed by his history of medical trauma and unfazed by what tomorrow may bring; *an aura of peace*—even at the depths of his most challenging moments, Oliver always seemed to be at peace with himself and with the world; *lack of focus on the material*—Oliver's preference for his cashmere sweaters over his wools was based solely on utility, not fashion or status. His cashmeres simply kept him warmer.

Clan Leader, Professor, Zen Master—truly a renaissance man . . . but with two extra legs.

Chapter Ten

Of Myths and Miracles

Days 33-34

VIRTUALLY ALL MAMMALS—WILD AND domesticated—communicate with each other, but often in ways that we humans are not able to decipher. Cheetahs have a range of vocalizations—chirping when trying to find each other; snarling or coughing as a sign of anger; churring to signal a social invitation; and purring by a mother to tell her cubs that the coast is clear to follow.

Quite a few years ago, I decided that it would be an absolute shame for the highway of my communication with Oliver to be a one-way street, limited to mundane master-to-canine commands such as *outside, dinner, stay, no, come*—or even such custom-tailored phrases as *lacka-walka*. Since Oliver is such an erudite fellow with so much to offer those who are willing to listen to his pearls of wisdom, I figured that the only sensible thing to do was to ascribe to him a mythical voice so that we could carry on two-way conversations that would run the gamut from the sublime to the ridiculous.

At first blush, this might seem absurd, but I figured it was just a distant dialectic cousin of the way in which parents often change their voices to ones of infantile-sounding gibberish when talking to a baby. I just decided to take it one step further and imbue Oliver with the ability to speak (admittedly through my mouth) in his own voice, to an extent that matched mine in terms of the bandwidth of our vocabulary and the range of topics on which we were conversant. All that remained was to choose an accent that fit his personality, so I adopted a patois that sounded like a cross-species blend between a small junkyard dog and a grizzled New York cabbie—but with the erudition of a creature who had often strolled the Commons at Yale and the lovely plot of earth in front of Langdell Hall at Harvard Law.

In our mano-a-cano conversations, Oliver often resorted to graphic and salty language whenever the situation warranted. Also, Ollie suffered from a distinct inability to pronounce certain letter combinations that I thought would be difficult for him ("th" was always pronounced as a "d" or a hard "t"—*this* became "*dis*" and *thought* became "*taught*"). I recall one evening as Ollie and I were walking around the duck-filled pond on our last constitutional of the day when the big fellow observed rather philosophically (through my moving lips), "When I was rescued from dat parking lot as a puppy, I never taught I'd have it so good . . . but goddamn if I don't deserve it." Ahhh, salt of the earth!

Mythical as this vocalization may seem, it's good to bear in mind that myths are the first cousins of miracles—same universe, just a different area code. And as we passed the thirty-fourth day in Oliver's one-hundred-day odyssey, I thought about another "thirty-fourth" that was reminiscent of the Miracle Man's saga. The movie classic *Miracle on 34th Street* recounts the tale of a character named Kris Kringle and the drama that surrounds whether or not Kris is indeed the real Santa Claus. In the end, it is the *believers* who triumph, the ones—young and old—who believe in the miracle of this white-bearded fellow.

With his own white goatee and salt-and-pepper hair, Oliver bore an uncanny resemblance to Kris, except that his girth was not nearly as portly. But as in the movie classic, I had wrapped the mantle of a legend around Oliver—and soon believed in miracles myself. The dialogue that we would pretend emanated from his mouth was just a fanciful way to feed the legend, but his survival as a foundling puppy and later on when deadly diseases attacked his twenty-pound body was grist for the legend mill that added a note of gravitas.

Over the years, fantasy and legend morphed into reality. The subtle ways in which my body language and verbal cues trickled down to the clan bestowed upon him a sense of leadership and invincibility, as all the four-legged and two-legged creatures in the Haas family accepted the fact that there was something truly special about Oliver. Perhaps it was the fact that like many of our heroes, fictional and real, Oliver discovered the alchemy for spinning triumph out of adversity—and each time our boy would do so, the legend grew.

Chapter Eleven

Forever Young

Days 35-40

PERHAPS SINGING IN THE RAIN WAS A PROMENADE to fame for the elegant dancer-actor Gene Kelly, but walking in the rain had always been distasteful to Oliver. Even when we bundled him up in his handsome yellow rain-slicker, Ollie would normally just stare out the open screen door at the puddles in his dog run, do an abrupt about-face, head back to his pillow-bed, and wait for the shower to pass. Although it might have been the Haas family aversion to a bad hair day, I suspect that in Oliver's case it had more to do with his distaste for wet feet. Even when we encouraged him to take care of business, Ollie would just stare back at us with an expression that seemed to say: "Look, no way am I going out der. I never, ever have an accident in the house, so I strongly prefer to wait until conditions are more to my liking. Besides, I never see *you* sitting on your commode when the bathroom is flooded."

On the morning of Day 36, in the midst of one of the longest spells of nonstop rain in recent Dallas history, I hitched Oliver up in his wheels and lifted him onto the walkway leading out to his favorite area. Despite the pounding rain and the flooded grassy squares that were his most targeted zones, surprisingly Ollie just trotted along with water careening off his spinning wheels. I detected no aversion whatsoever to the drenched surfaces or to the fact that his paws were thoroughly wet. Even his back legs that were lifted into the stirrups to prevent any scraping of his delicate toes were soaked to the bone. But Ollie didn't seem to mind at all—our boy was moving and that's all that mattered. A regular Gene Kelly—*sans* umbrella!

Scooting in the rain was not the only maneuver that our boy added to his repertoire in the sixth week out of ICU. Oliver had figured out how to literally turn the corner. One of the challenges for a wheel-assisted canine is learning that its back legs are suddenly wider than before, so that when it wants to turn a corner, it must swing further out to avoid one of the wheels bumping up against an obstacle in its path. For the first few weeks, Oliver would simply halt and wait when his chariot hit an obstruction—as if some invisible hand had reached out and stopped his forward progress. Eventually, Ollie began to learn that swinging wide around corners is a better approach, that obstacles need not always be confronted head on—a good lesson for him and perhaps too for the people in his inner circle.

Oliver may have profited from overhearing my incessant lectures to our daughters about life lessons. I've stressed, over and over again, that life is like a game of baseball: we are often thrown curveballs that are hard to anticipate and harder yet to hit, but we must learn to adjust to even the most wicked curveballs if we wish to thrive, simply because that's the nature of the game we're in. I've tried to point out that the game never ends until the lights are turned off and we head to the dugout for the last time. But until then, we must learn to handle those curveballs, we learn not to complain that the game is unfair, and we learn that the obstacles are part of the playing field—like Oliver, we learn how to turn the corner and move on.

On Day 38, when we had all retired for the night to the master bed and there were twenty paws stretched out in the sack alongside Candice and me, I glanced over at Ollie and noticed something about the profile of his head and the way the dim light cast a shadow over his face that gave him the appearance of being eerily old. I ruffled his fur and kissed him a few times until he drew his head back in a gesture of annoyance, and the aura of being a very, very old guy was dispelled.

Once again, I was free to harbor the childish wish that Ollie would live forever and to deceive myself into forgetting—for just a moment—that the bargain was for only one hundred days. After that, I had no reason to complain about the fact that Oliver too was mortal.

But live forever we do not. And yet, a few of the most gifted in our midst do have the power to challenge Father Time and emerge with some claim to victory. Several years ago during a photo shoot in northern Argentina, when my helicopter was grounded by foul weather, I curled up with a parade of cups of strong coffee and read an entire book by Peter Feist on the life of the great French artist Pierre-Auguste Renoir. The account of his life was most inspiring, particularly the part that focused on Renoir's struggle to be productive in his final years. It triggered in my mind the thought of how each of us will one day answer the question, "When did you produce your best work?"

It's a haunting question. When the time comes to look back from the imposed comfort of old age when little else is expected, and we are all alone with our thoughts, how will each of us answer that question? If the Olympian heights of our lives have been defined by athletic prowess, will we point to a time when only two decades or less had registered on our life clock? If the supreme act of birthing and rearing children was our defining opus, when did the product of our labors become so self-sufficient that our best work was clearly behind us?

What about the artist who refuses to detach the paintbrush from his hand until the very end or scrape the clay from his fingernails for the last time? There must be sharp delight in answering, "I don't know . . . perhaps my best work is yet to come." I am always fascinated by the lives of great artists whose genius spans decades and leaves an imprint on rotating generations of audiences.

The example of the luminary Pierre-Auguste Renoir is one of the most striking. Renoir apprenticed as a porcelain painter at the tender age of thirteen, took up open-air painting in his twenties, and eventually evolved into one of the timeless masters of French Impressionism. But perhaps Renoir's life is best defined by his tenacious refusal to acknowledge that his best work was behind him. At the age of thirty-nine, after achieving notoriety as a great Impressionist, Renoir broke his right arm and taught himself to paint with his left. Afterward, Renoir suffered successive bouts of rheumatoid arthritis, causing facial and arm paralysis—but the artist continued to produce work that captivates audiences more than one hundred years later.

At the age of seventy, confined to a wheelchair with only a few years of life remaining in a body wracked with pain, the aging master managed to have the paintbrush attached to his crippled hand with pieces of string. Renoir coupled his lofty genius with wry humor that offered a priceless glimpse into the psyche of this very human creature, reputed to have once said: "One morning one of us had run out of black; and that was the birth of Impressionism."

The word *admire* does not do justice to the awe that such life stories arouse in me. There is exquisite nobility in the refusal of the incredibly few Renoirs among us who continue to evolve and push forward relentlessly, undaunted by the debilitating conditions of old age, disease, or even fame and fortune. Chased by an inner drive that will not allow the paintbrush to rest on its palette, such immortal mortals display an overwhelming beauty in their staunch unwillingness to answer the question, "When did you produce your best work?"

For the noble creatures among us—grounded on two legs or on four—who refuse to bend to the hands of time or the palsy of crippling injury, youth is a state of mind and aging is for others.

Chapter Twelve

Uneasy Lies the Head
That Wears a Crown

Days 41-45

"Uneasy lies the head that wears a crown."
—William Shakespeare

SHAKESPEARE GOT IT EXACTLY RIGHT IN THAT classic line from Henry IV, Part II. Leadership—whether of a royal family or an investment firm or a canine clan—is a lonely occupation. That crown may be the object of lifelong ambition or all-consuming envy, but once it is placed squarely on your head, its ponderous weight may become much more imposing than was ever anticipated. Shakespeare also chose the right venue for writing about imperial schemes—I doubt that any country has offered up more scandalous or salacious palace intrigues than mother England. Even to this day, we are titillated by the conspiracy theories and clandestine affairs that have spilled barrels of ink onto the tabloids that trumpet each twist of plot in this real-life soap opera.

I've often wondered whether Prince Charles—forever in the royal family photo but never the central figure—must not feel ambivalent about his mother Queen Elizabeth's health and longevity. Here is the Prince of Wales in his early sixties just tapping his foot, waiting for the day when all his grooming to be King of England will finally morph from dress rehearsal to showtime—but Elizabeth shows neither the inclination nor the failing health that augurs well for the realization of the Prince's ambitions any time soon.

Across the pond over here in the States, I have no doubt that there were moments when our own Henry (a rather royal British name) felt the same way about Oliver. Of all the other guys in the clan, only Henry exhibited a wide streak of alpha—a nascent clan leader consigned to the role of biding his time in the wings of Oliver's theater.

Henry had always been a remarkable physical specimen, a dashingly handsome cocka-poo, who was about as regal-looking as any half-breed could be. Tight blond curls covered his entire muscular body with a long tail that had the most elegant sweep to it. Henry was endowed with a physique that offered the perfect blend of raw strength, stamina, and athleticism. Always the favorite with our daughters' boyfriends for his indefatigable playfulness, Henry would keep wrestling and fetching until the boys had had enough. Try to take one of his toys away and Henry would wrap his front legs around that toy so tightly that you could hoist him up in the air by lifting the toy and swing him around like a carousel.

In their younger and sprier days, Henry and Oliver had quite a few donnybrooks, particularly in the master bedroom, where the precise placement of canine bodies on the bed seemed to elicit their most aggressive and competitive behavior. The choicest positions of all were at the head of the bed, closest to the ultimate alpha male and female. A fracas between Oliver and Henry could erupt at any moment and escalate in a matter of seconds into a no-holds-barred brawl. At the outbreak of hostilities, Candice would shriek in utter panic, and I would be left to separate the two rivals. As Oliver's physical condition deteriorated, Henry stepped up the level of aggression, but the younger brother never quite managed to tip the Miracle Man off his throne. On a few occasions, fur would fly and blood would trickle until the two were physically separated, but not once did Oliver retreat from the field of battle—and the scepter was never handed off to his upstart brother.

When I intervened to impose a cease-fire on the warring factions, I would normally grab Henry by his two rear legs and yank him back from the clenched tangle of paws and jaws. I suppose that might have advantaged Oliver somewhat, who was then in a position to deliver the parting shot, but I was concerned for Ollie's welfare in what I never considered to be a particularly fair fight. Henry was younger and stronger, and Oliver had a tough time even focusing on the fisticuffs with his incipient blindness. Henry knew that

I was there to protect Oliver, and I always felt a bit guilty afterward that there was an element of favoritism behind my intervention.

But all that eventually passed. In a strange twist of fate, Henry was assaulted by an immune-mediated disease very similar to Oliver's platelet and neuropathy attacks. Whereas Ollie's immune system went haywire in taking aim at the clotting agents in his blood and then the neural connections to his muscles, Henry's laid him low with an immensely painful arthritic condition that literally stopped him in his tracks.

With Henry down, we responded with both heavy doses of steroids to fight off his condition and constant helpings of TLC to comfort his first encounter with a serious illness. Compounding the intense arthritic pain was a ligament rupture in his knee that was nearly unbearable all by itself. For months, Henry needed to be carried up and down the stairs and kept on a leash while all the other guys (Oliver excluded) roamed the property at will.

Perhaps feeling the guilt of having favored his old nemesis from those battles of years past, I lavished affection and attention on Henry that equaled the tenderness offered up to Oliver during his health crises—and we bonded as never before. For the first time in his life, this immensely tough and physical guy needed hands-on attention just to navigate his way around the house and conduct his business outside. In his very expressive eyes, I could see that Henry knew that this time I was there to protect him.

Love has a way of evolving over time, often most dramatically in response to challenges faced together, and this medical challenge was a game-changer in terms of my relationship with Henry. Even though I could feel my own physical and mental fatigue sink in at the end of the more frantic days of caring for both Oliver and Henry, it was the good type of exhaustion. I was expending energy for a worthy cause; I was coming to my sons' aid. As strange as it sounds, I just knew that Henry appreciated what I was doing for him during his most vulnerable days.

Oliver loved his *lacka-walkas* and Henry did as well, but both guys were consigned to the Disabled List in the aftermath of their respective bouts with paralysis and knee surgery, so a no-holds-barred scamper was out of the question. As I tried to figure out how to engineer a *lacka-walka* for two geriatric four-leggers with their own peculiar medical challenges, the thought crossed my mind that in a perverse way, my long-harbored wish to become a veterinarian had almost been granted—and without the drudgery of long years of study or the outrageous tuition bills of vet school. I was becoming a reluctant expert in the care and recovery of injured canines.

On Day 43, I decided to give the two boys another option for roaming the property, attaching one end of a dual-clip leash to Ollie and the other to Henry, letting the two move in tandem around the lake with only a modicum of supervision. With Henry as the tractor and Ollie and his scooter as the trailer, this duo negotiated the property magnificently. Henry was able to maneuver virtually at will, and Ollie had a power boost in Henry's ability to haul the scooter through the thicker vegetation. Except for my occasionally holding the middle of the two-pronged leash to prevent Ollie from rolling over the lake embankment, it worked like a charm with minimal human intervention.

There is something emotionally powerful about two old rivals eventually forgoing their history of armed conflict and finding comfort in each other's company. At long last, Oliver and Henry had become kindred spirits as each one fought back from a crippling injury to regain his mobility. All the rivalry for the thorny crown of clan leadership had disappeared, all the tension was gone. Facing the infirmities of advancing age, each was locked in his own valiant battle with a common enemy. Just like two boxers who have staged an epic series of magnificent encounters (a version of Ali-Frazier but with eight legs), Ollie and Henry were elder statesmen who had patched up their differences and let a shared brotherhood become the fulcrum of their relationship. As we wound our way around the lake, I could almost feel the respect that the two harbored for each other, now that there was nothing left to prove.

Chapter Thirteen

Small Steps

Days 46-56

THE END OF A LONG JOURNEY—I WAS ON THE cusp of achieving a mission hatched in the storied halls of National Geographic to retrace the icy footprints of the Vikings and become the first to photograph the wide expanse of the Arctic from above. Three years of photography, seven countries that spanned the northern band of the world from eastern Scandinavia to western Alaska, fourteen multi-week treks into the Arctic, and close to seventy-five thousand images—at last, it was time to bring my adventure to a close.

When I first conceived the project almost four years before, I was drawn to a part of the world that beckoned as the ultimate challenge—a region so vast and so beset by harsh climate as to pose a logistical gauntlet for an aerial artist and a personal nightmare for someone who dreaded the cold as much as I did. Whenever I conjured up images of the Arctic, words such as *hostile* and *barren* and *primitive* and *inhospitable* came to mind. I had overcome my fear of heights only to enter another theater where I needed to brace myself for an encore performance.

But now it was almost over, and the cold was dreaded no more. It had become a warm and cozy place for someone who had entered its realm and been treated as a guest almost always is by the inhabitants of the far north, as a fellow traveler deserving of gracious hospitality. All that remained was the fourteenth trip, a two-week photo shoot in northern Canada where polar bears would be the main attraction—no more challenging than several of its thirteen predecessors in terms of weather and logistics, but it would be my first shoot away from Oliver after his accident.

For whatever reason, I never found the physical separation from my two-legged family members to be cause for anguish or anxiety on the eve of a long shoot. Not that I wasn't intensely lonely at times as I pursued my artistic passions in some of the most remote places on Earth, but I was simply not preoccupied with the thought that the family wouldn't be reunited after a brief separation. Or more accurately, knowing that I would be the one dangling out of helicopters, it just never occurred to me that the members of my family would be the ones at risk of not being there when it was time for us to be reunited.

But as the Arctic project unfolded, I found myself becoming more and more anxious about Oliver's surviving during my times in the field. My travels had often been bookends around his latest health crisis, either right before or right after the most recent episode. The thought always haunted me as I was packing my gear for an upcoming shoot that I might be seeing Oliver for the last time. It was a gut-wrenching feeling that repeated itself with every trip to the Arctic. As each crisis came and went in his thickening medical portfolio, the good-byes became ever more melancholy—and the returning embraces ever more emotional. Each day when e-mail or voice connectivity was available, Candice always gave an "all's well with Oliver and the gang" report to my enormous relief.

As physically spent as I was from the drain of bouncing back and forth between the Arctic and the States and the tightrope walk of balancing my investment career and this photographic venture, it would nevertheless be a time for celebration once this last trip was over and the final images were "in the can." I had gone eyeball-to-eyeball against the logistical setbacks and the extremes of weather that such an enterprise entails, but I had survived. And Oliver had performed just as splendidly in surviving in his own bailiwick—our boy had started three years earlier with full sight and the use of all four legs and had ended up a still noble creature for whom sensing the world and navigating in his own little piece of it was an evolving adventure.

As I carefully packed up my arsenal of photo gear and stuffed my duffel bags with battered cold-weather apparel for this last shoot, I was even more anxious than usual. We were just about halfway into our one-hundred-day journey, and I could not help but think that I was deserting my companion on a trek that I had pledged we would undertake together. Not surprisingly, it was Oliver who rescued me from my funk.

On the last night before I headed off to the frozen tundra of Canada, Oliver gave me a good-bye present, one that would ease my longing for him over the next two weeks. On his final walk of the night, after Candice and I balanced him on all fours simply to test the strength of his back legs and give him a suitable business position, Ollie took a few tentative steps for the very first time since his accident. It may not have been far, but it was walking—three short steps on all fours and then his derrière floating gently back to Earth to our thunderous applause.

Who knew where it would go from there? In Oliver's world of recovery from paralysis and the threat that lung disease would bring him down, walking again—even just a few steps—only seven weeks after his release from ICU was the equivalent in my eyes of Wilbur and Orville Wright's achievement at Kitty Hawk in 1903. The Wright brothers' flight lasted only twelve seconds, but it nevertheless was the first powered flight by man. Ever the Professor, that night Oliver reminded us all that events need not last long to qualify as miracles. What a memory to pack in my already stuffed duffel bags and take along for fourteen days!

Over the next two weeks, I would travel thousands of miles to places in the Canadian far north with names like Saskatoon, Stony Rapids, Athabasca, Cluff Mine, Fort Chipewyan, and Churchill—and there would indeed be times when I was terribly lonely for the Miracle Man and his clan. But I thought of those steps over and over again. The image of him walking was just like a box of Godiva chocolates—whenever I felt the urge, I would head to that box and savor the image of Ollie on all fours, delivering another of his miracles.

But the occasional trip to the chocolate box was not a panacea for the entire two-week hiatus. Perhaps it was the frustration imposed by blustery weather that often brought my aerial exploits to a grinding halt, or perhaps it was because I spent so much time waiting to track polar bears that were desperate for Hudson Bay to finally freeze over and provide a launching pad for seal hunts. For whatever reason, I passed a great deal of my idle time in this venue doing the same thing that its native inhabitants and four-legged creatures have done for generations—thinking about survival—the most elemental struggles that man and beast endure against the biblical forces of nature and the tiniest, but just as deadly, forces of disease that ricochet inside their bodies. Even when the weather abated and we were able to lift off in the few crevices of light and calm winds that we found, the theme of survival continued to infuse my work.

I spent the majority of my time in the air searching for polar bears, a magnificent creature locked in battle with the consequences of climate change in its own efforts to survive. And in that struggle, the very western edge of Hudson Bay where we were camped in late October is one of the prime battlegrounds. At this precise time of year each autumn, the polar bears of Manitoba Province converge to await the first wave of frozen ice in the Bay. The small town of Churchill is considered by many to be the epicenter of central Canada's polar bear country. In late October, the lower recesses of Hudson Bay—composed mostly of fresh water from the network of rivers that empty into it—freeze first, before the saltier upper regions of the Bay. As the water transforms to ice normally in the last two weeks of October, the polar bears of Manitoba gather in the immediate vicinity of Churchill to begin their long-awaited trek out onto the fresh ice where ringed seals, their culinary mainstay, await the great white hunters of the north. Given the bears' limited ability to swim long distances, the newly formed ice is the platform that enables them to pursue the seals. Males are aching to regain the hundreds of pounds of fat and muscle shed during the past several months, and females with cubs are just as anxious to do the same, as survival of the young hangs in a precarious balance. But this year, there was no ice at the edges of the Bay—winter was late in arriving and the ravenous bears were at risk.

Normally at this time of year, the frigid temperatures and cool winds that accompany the onset of winter are virtually guaranteed to clear the skies—ideal photography weather. But the word *guarantee* never belongs in the same sentence with a description of Arctic weather. The weather all week in Churchill had been dreadful—warmer than normal with fog and rain that delayed the freezing of the ice and nearly shut down our aerial exploits. The bears kept edging toward the Bay but were simply lounging around, barely moving so as not to waste any of the precious reserves of energy in their depleted tanks.

With idle time and idle hands that only rarely gripped my cameras, my thoughts inevitably turned to Oliver and his own struggle for survival over the past two months. With Oliver's small but steady moves away from the edge of the precipice, I was at last permitted the luxury of collapsing just a bit emotionally—I must have figured that I had earned the right to find a small sense of relief in my own momentary weakness. Stationed in a remote locale that was ever fixated on survival, my mind often drifted back to the darkest moments of the past fifty days when Oliver was barely clinging to life and one of the vets was gently urging that we consider all our options. I thought about the vet's admonition to think of the animal first if it came down to a decision about sustaining his life beyond a certain point. But even then, every instinct in my body resisted the notion that we were anywhere near the point of not allowing Oliver to continue his struggle.

In this preoccupation with survival, I often thought about how as masters we are sometimes given the awful choice of whether to allow our companions to live or die. I thought about how we humans are prone to substitute our judgment for theirs when trying to ascertain whether a dog's life is worth preserving beyond a certain point of physical deterioration—whether its quality of life has sunk below the point where the "merciful" thing to do is to "put it down" (a curious phrase, as if we were talking about laying the evening newspaper down on the kitchen table, when in fact "down" means down to stay).

With the benefit of some distance from the worst of Oliver's dark days, I thought about how owners are destined to face that awesome judgment call in the midst of what must be a state of emotional turmoil. In reaching such a decision, I've always believed that we must avoid the temptation to visualize what we would feel if our plight were the same as theirs—our own litmus test should really be not whether we would wish to move on in such circumstances but rather whether the animal desires to move on with life even though its circumstances are compromised and its limitations are severe. And yet, the anguish of the decision is often compounded by the economic reality that the family simply cannot afford the outlandish medical bills that accompany its heroic efforts to keep the family pet alive . . . and the four-legger is in no position to comfort the family by saying, "It's all right; I'm ready to move on." If the economic realities are overwhelming, the family is left with no choice but to intervene, knowing that it was the only practical decision but nevertheless harboring a tinge of guilt that dollars may have trumped life.

Animals have an uncanny ability, quite often superior to our own, to adjust and survive, to redefine a "good life" as circumstances warrant. If I were blinded by cataracts, my life would be drastically altered—I would certainly not be able to carry on with my passion for photography. But for Ollie his near total loss of sight had not proven to be "mission critical"—his acute sense of smell enabled his nose to step forward and be his primary periscope on the world around him. And the fact that Ollie was strapped to a scooter did not amount to proof of anything at all about his quality of life. Ollie always sauntered about deliberately and with the utmost dignity, not with the leash-straining gusto of a dog just aching to chase squirrels.

I have seen plenty of animals in the wild cling tenaciously to life far beyond the point where we would consider pressing on—lions mauled in a fight for pride hegemony who limp away and yet live to fight another day, or zebras with strips of hide ripped from their torso by an attacking predator, but nevertheless trotting along with the herd.

I once witnessed—and photographed—a pack of wild dogs in the African savanna that included two severely injured members, one with a broken leg and the other with a snare trap of barbed wire wrapped tightly around its lacerated chest. No longer able to join in the hunt, the two were nevertheless able to "babysit" the youngsters when the main pack was away on a hunt and protect the defenseless pups from wandering into turf controlled by larger predators. After a successful kill, the hunters invariably brought back enough raw meat for everyone, carrying the tasty morsels in the "lunch pail" of their bellies and then regurgitating for the dining pleasure of the pups and the two babysitters. In the melee that followed, with sharp teeth chewing fresh meat, tails were wagging furiously and eyes gleaming in the rich African sunlight, and the injured were indistinguishable from the full-fledged hunters—all seemed equally content with the joys of being alive. That joy was exquisitely obvious in the tails that whipped back and forth and in the eyes that seemed to spray shafts of light outward just as much as they absorbed the sun's rays coming in.

And so it was with Ollie. The tail and the eyes told it all. Strolling along in his scooter, his tail held high and flapping side to side with every step, there was absolutely nothing in that image that would merit the word *crippled* or *pitiful* in its caption—that label would be so foreign from the spirit that propelled his every step. And as if that were not proof enough, his eyes—though clouded over with milky cataracts—spoke their own language to those of us willing to listen: "*I am not just clinging to life; I am relishing it and embracing it.*" This was a creature who was not about to relinquish the struggle for survival or allow anyone else to call a halt to his own adventures.

Chapter Fourteen

Kindred Spirits

Days 57-60

THE DISTANT SHORELINE OF HUDSON BAY IS
hardly the place where you would expect to find Oliver's
kindred spirits. While his clan had been assembled from all
over the States, Ollie's sphere of influence and kinship had
not been known to extend across international borders—
at least not until the final few days of the photo shoot in
Manitoba Province.

Oliver is obviously not the only sight-challenged canine in
the world and certainly not the only miracle creature on four
legs. In the final few days of the photo shoot, we were to meet
another who qualified in both categories. I was holed up with
my daughter Samme (who doubled as my photo assistant) in
a small bed-and-breakfast in Churchill. The cozy B&B was
also home to a group of eighteen malamute-huskies—all but
two of which were sheltered off premises—that were a blend

of working sled dogs and cherished family members cared for by the husband-and-wife proprietors of the B&B.

As in the days when our ancestors first discovered thousands of years ago that man and dog together could enhance each other's chances of survival with complementary skills, in this lodge in Churchill, the symbiotic bond between human and canine flourished once again. Sled dog teams are a major attraction for visitors to this small Hudson Bay community of eight hundred, which draws thousands of tourists each year to witness the congregating of the polar bears that venture onto the first wave of frozen ice in the Bay. The chance to be whisked around the surrounding area by the sled dog teams operated by this B&B was a major feature that the lodge employed to fill its guest rooms night after night during peak season. And the proprietors reciprocated by catering to the needs of the dogs with food and shelter and generous rations of affection.

The most famous member of the clan was certainly Isabel, a classic-looking ten-year-old retired sled dog that I had the pleasure of babysitting one afternoon between aerial shooting sequences. Isabel was totally blind and in need of occasional adult supervision, since there were stairs and other possible pitfalls around the B&B. Just like her very distant cousin Oliver, Isabel had learned that a keen sense of smell and mental mapping of a familiar area will send signals to the brain that partially replace the more direct sense of sight. Amazingly, Isabel had, until recently, continued to be part of the working team even without the benefit of sight, as the sound of her master's "Mush!" and the feel of being strapped into the harness with her teammates were enough to goad her into action in a place where polar bears still roam free. The thought of Isabel in her harness and Oliver in his scooter, neither one sighted but both able to navigate their own chunk of the world, was a parallel vision that readily came to mind.

While I was working away on the second floor of the B&B during my babysitting stint, Isabel walked up and down the very narrow stairway close to a dozen times to continually seek assurance that she was not alone. The first few times I escorted her back down the stairs, but eventually it was clear that she needed no help at all. With thoughts of a similarly challenged Oliver in my head, we bonded almost immediately, particularly after I offered Isabel all the affection and clandestine snacks that she clearly craved.

Even though she was only able to see the world in a way different from the sighted, Isabel was every bit as enthralled with life as I had always assumed Oliver to be. While I could certainly be accused of convincing myself to view Oliver's life as more fulfilled than it actually may have been, I was in a position to be more objective about this retired sled dog. I was only invested with a few days' worth of affection for Isabel—but, like Oliver, she was clearly one very contented creature who snatched hefty chunks of pleasure out of each day she was alive.

Spending a gentle afternoon babysitting a blind sled dog is one way to celebrate Oliver's kinship with his Canadian brethren, but rescuing a damsel in distress is quite another.

The preamble for this rescue mission began the day before our departure from Canada, in the midst of a whiteout that engulfed Churchill. It was one of those blustery snowstorms where, propelled by ferocious winds, the snow actually appeared to be moving sideways, defying any intention of ever landing on the ground. We had totally abandoned any thought of lifting off in our helicopter for another aerial flip, in favor of checking with the airlines to see whether commercial flights were expected to resume operations any time soon.

Even though the wind was howling nonstop, Samme swore she heard the constant whimpering of a dog behind the B&B. Undeterred by either the blizzard or the fact that there might be polar bears wandering in the vicinity, Samme ventured outside and returned with a drenched bundle of wriggling fur in her arms. Perhaps she had not exactly committed an act of outright dog-napping, but Samme's version of how she had secured permission from the neighbor to unchain this puppy from its stake in the ice-packed backyard was short on details. Even though this creature was in serious need of a day at the beauty shop, the resemblance to a very young Oliver was uncanny—she was a long-haired mixed breed with a black-and-white coat and large round eyes that could light a lantern.

This rambunctious gal (her gender determined after close inspection) either knew a savior when she sniffed one or just couldn't take another night in that abysmal weather—either way, her enthusiasm for Samme and anyone Samme seemed to know was boundless. Indiscriminate wet kisses and the thwacking of her thumping tail were distributed all around the B&B. But at the end of the night, the dog was not ours to keep, and Samme reluctantly trudged over to return the precious parcel. Afterward, Samme was inconsolable and insisted that we were not leaving Churchill without one last-ditch effort at rescuing the puppy. With her superficial resemblance to Oliver and the fact that she might not survive much longer in such weather, I was easily converted into a willing accomplice in Samme's nefarious scheme.

After we protested to local authorities, the pup was taken inside for the night by the neighbor, who it turned out was not the real owner after all. The owner was away overnight in a small town outside Churchill and had left his home and the dog in the so-called care of this other man. At 8:30 on the morning of our departure from Canada, I ventured out to the nearby home of a relative of the owner, from where I was able to reach him by phone. After appealing to his long-extinct sympathies and waving two hundred dollars in cold hard cash at the voice on the other end of the line, we had a deal. We were the proud new owners of a nameless puppy who could have passed for Oliver's baby sister.

Within another two hours, we knocked off a rather prodigious checklist—dog crate and leash borrowed from neighbors, veterinarian in Winnipeg (our first stop on the way home) lined up for an exam, and crate-with-rescued-puppy-inside loaded onboard the flight to Winnipeg. Five hours later, our newfound bundle had been examined and inoculated by the vet in Winnipeg and pronounced in reasonably good health even though underweight and dehydrated. The Winnipeg vet marveled at the fact that this roughly eight-month-old puppy had survived outdoors in conditions that would have caused winter-hardened huskies five times her size to seek shelter from the elements. After a hurried exit from the vet's office, she was whisked back to the Winnipeg airport to join Samme on a flight to Montreal, where she received what must have been the first bath of her young life at a dog-friendly Holiday Inn. The following morning, Nameless Puppy became a U.S. citizen as Samme touched down at New York's LaGuardia Airport, and our rescue saga came to a glorious end almost precisely twenty-four hours after it began.

In a fitting sequel to this Horatio Alger story, Gracie (nameless no more) became a pampered doyenne of the New York arts scene after her adoption by an enormously kindhearted executive of one of the most prominent museums on the Upper East Side. Gracie was destined to spend most of her weekdays at the museum as the real-life heroine of a daring rescue mission, having barely escaped the open jaws of a wild polar bear (not literally true, but with the benefit of time and distance, the rescue legend grew to near mythic proportions).

The resemblance to Oliver was clearly more than fur-deep—one rescued from the parking lot of an abandoned apartment building and the other from the frozen tundra of

Canada—both neglected for the first few months of their lives but never to know another day of want.

At last, the final shoot in Canada was over, and the Arctic odyssey was history. What began two weeks earlier for one distinguished elder statesman with his taking a few tentative steps in Dallas ended for another—fourteen years his junior—with a leisurely stroll through Central Park.

Chapter Fifteen

Hitting Stride

Days 61-65

THE ONE COMMON DENOMINATOR AMONG ALL my aerial projects over the past eight years has been the unexpected. Regardless of how meticulously I plan each shoot and the volumes of research that I pore over in advance of venturing onto new turf, nothing ever quite prepares me for the sights or the challenges that I encounter—nor have I ever completed a project with anything resembling my preconceived notions of the region I was about to set foot on. The Arctic proved to be no exception.

On the last night of the final trip of the Arctic excursion, as I was carelessly gathering up clothing that deserved to be incinerated upon my return and delicately packing camera gear that had earned its rightful place as cherished hardware in my artistic arsenal, I allowed myself to feel a measure of pride in what had been accomplished. I knew that I had overcome my fear of a frigid realm that tested me to the limits and permitted no margin for error. And in the process, I emerged with images that captured a small fraction of the inherent beauty and bold diversity that permeates this part of the world. I walked away not only as a survivor but also as a great admirer of the Arctic: its peerless majesty, its hardy inhabitants, and its iconic wildlife. It was as if I had become close friends with a pit bull that I had feared all these years, only to discover that this breed was every bit as deserving of love as any other and just as willing to reciprocate with tenderness and affection.

I also experienced a very different feeling being away from Oliver on this trip than the one I had anticipated. I fully expected that the gray mist of loneliness would gradually descend over my moods and that each day would seem longer than the one before. Part of the loneliness of being away from the clan had always been the inability to explain in advance exactly where I was going or how long I'd be gone. All of the guys except Ollie were able to quickly fill the very small vacuum created by my absence with the attention of others and the comfort of daily routines. But Oliver and I were so tightly wound together in a helix of emotions that the vacuum was not so easily filled—for him or for me—by anything or anyone else. Particularly in light of the crisis that Ollie had just barely weathered, I thought this particular trip to Canada might be the loneliest of all. But it never shaped up that way.

I suppose that in the past my loneliness had been partly fueled by fear of another unexpected crisis cropping up in my absence, whereas this time the crisis had already reared its head and Ollie had proven to be equal to the task. Instead of trepidation for the unknown, I left home with a sense of confidence in the already known—Oliver had stared down this crisis and was clearly on the mend. And I had healed with him; the emotional scar tissue of having almost lost him was no longer a source of sharp pain. Like most scars, it was still visible but not nearly so sensitive anymore.

During the two weeks when I was shuttling around the Canadian far north, Ollie exhibited impressive progress in his rehabilitation. The tangible signs of recovery continued to emerge on an almost daily basis: advancing in his hydrotherapy tank from eleven to thirteen straight minutes of vigorous trotting; extending his unassisted four-legged stand from thirty seconds to one full minute; executing a long series of sit-to-stands with almost no assistance (except the temptation of a treat strategically placed a few inches in front of his outstretched nose); and perhaps most dramatic of all, lifting up one of his back legs during hydrotherapy and placing his foot squarely on the moving treadmill for a few consecutive steps.

From my perspective, his exceptional progress over the past few weeks had been cause for both elation and fascination. The elation is easy to understand: our boy was clearly moving in the right direction, adapting well to his scooter-assisted locomotion, building up his forward body strength, and showing signs that there might yet be further improvement.

The fascination with his progress was more intriguing—unraveling the mystery of why Oliver continued to exert himself to the limits of his endurance and his neural capacity. His recovery had already achieved a remarkable state of equilibrium—clan leadership intact, mobility restored via the scooter, and his attitude clearly in a good place. Oliver could simply have trundled along in the hydrotherapy tank for twelve or even thirteen minutes and built up his cardio endurance and his front leg strength, on which his mobility depended.

But that simply wasn't enough for him. Without any prodding or external incentive for the Herculean task of lifting up that back leg, something inside Oliver released a sudden burst of determination to take that small step forward with the pad of his back foot squarely on the moving belt. Was it instinct, a preprogrammed pattern from his ancestral heritage seeking to restore motion in order to hunt and survive? Or was it something else? Exactly why did Oliver urge his brain to send just a few more volts of current through the constricted highway of his spinal cord down to his leg and ask for that foot to be lifted?

We will never know for sure. But what we do know is that in the span of just over eight weeks, Oliver had transformed himself from a dog confined to his bed waiting to be lifted up by one of his human handlers, to a fellow who whipped around in his scooter, stood on all fours for a minute at a time, performed in the hydrotherapy tank with the vigor of a much younger guy, and walked a few steps on his own, sometimes with a back foot down on a moving treadmill. No miracle drugs had achieved any of this—only a small fourteen-year-old package of intelligence and fierce determination that had earned the handle *Miracle Man*.

At last, after two weeks in the Arctic, it was time to see Oliver again. Nothing quite prepares me for my first impression upon seeing someone after a period of separation, even one as brief as just a few weeks. My imagination always seems to play tricks on me, and I tend to visualize someone much younger or fitter or somehow very different. If the separation has been for an extended period of time, a child appears to have grown up overnight, and a middle-aged man seems to have spawned thinning gray hair that instantly replaces the thick black locks I recall from our last meeting only a few years back.

But this had only been two weeks. And yet, there still seemed to be something different about Oliver—or perhaps it was in the way that I perceived him. On our first long walk around the lake together, I stared at Ollie's face and carefully examined his every step in the chariot. The overwhelming impression was one of contentment—Oliver was simply more at peace than I recalled. His struggles seemed to be more behind him than in front of him. It dawned on me that this guy was in a very good place . . . and knew it. The frustrations of limited mobility had largely been overcome through therapy and hard work. Ollie had been able to reach a fair compromise with his body parts under which walking with his scooter was a reasonable facsimile of how he walked before, and standing on all fours without wobbling as the wind whipped through his gray hair was no different than in days gone by.

At one point during our first morning constitutional together after my return, as I was examining the precise details of his movements, Oliver tilted his head in my direction, and I could almost hear him say, "Hey, Dad, lose the microscope! Don't expect a miracle every day. Just ease back, man, and don't forget that each day is its own miracle." Our boy was hitting stride—I was the one who needed to get in step.

Chapter Sixteen

Back in the Pool

Days 66-71

SO CLOSE, SO VERY CLOSE . . . I OFTEN UTTER those words when asked to describe my relationship with Oliver. But one night during the tenth week out of ICU, I used them with a very different meaning. A group of folks from our family and our daughter Vanessa's fiancé's family were sitting around at the très chic Soho House in Manhattan celebrating their engagement. Wine was flowing and music was blaring in this enclave of the young where the world outside seems to disappear in a cacophony of designer dresses, five-inch heels, and rough-shaven young male faces. It is a place to lose yourself or perhaps to find another who is similarly lost.

Candice and I were at least one generation away from the median age in Soho House, and by 11:00 p.m., as the crowd was just warming up to what would become a fever pitch three or four hours hence, we were winding down, craving the comfort and silence of our bed back at the hotel. I decided to retreat, at least mentally if not physically, from this mecca of Manhattan nightlife by scrolling through the pictures on my Blackberry, most of which were ones taken of Oliver in intensive care more than two months before. I shared the pictures with Candice, who shook her head and said, "Doesn't even look like the same dog!" In some of the photos, Ollie could barely lift his head; in others, his head was tilted up slightly but his body was attached to a maze of intravenous tubes and monitors that kept track of his vital signs. It was then that I said, "We were close, so very close." Candice knew exactly what I meant—close to the edge, close to losing him forever, close to never having the chance to count the days in our one-hundred-day journey.

A few hours earlier, a call from my assistant, Christine—who had to shout through the phone to be heard over the din of the luncheon crowd at Barney's—had triggered quite a different sense of closeness. Christine had taken Oliver to his weekly rehab session, and the Miracle Man had pushed the bar ever higher. Ollie had repeatedly gone from the sit position to a full four-legged stand totally on his own, as his back legs managed to hoist up the full weight of his sitting body. No therapist's hands to lift his back side, just a straightforward duel between the force of gravity and the determination in his back legs—Sir Isaac Newton versus Sir Oliver Winston Haas.

Even though I was burrowed in the canyons of New York more than one thousand miles away, I might as well have been in the rehab session with Oliver, beaming at the sight of my eldest son's achievements. It was at moments such as that when I allowed myself the luxury of thinking, *We are going to make it—we are destined to reach that one hundredth day together.* But that watershed moment was still one month away, and I had learned not to take anything for granted. After all, that was the whole point of cherishing every moment with Oliver.

From time to time, we are each presented with a reminder of our advancing age, and the weekend of engagement festivities in New York for Vanessa was all the reminder that my body needed. Candice and I dressed to the nines and partied with kids half our age until well after midnight two nights in a row. We were dancing and toasting neck-and-neck with members of the next gen set who marveled at how we could still cut a wicked path across the dance floor regardless of the vintage of the tunes. But once we arrived back in Dallas after the long flight home Sunday night, sore feet and aching backs that had mercifully gone into hibernation for the prior forty-eight hours emerged to claim control of our middle-aged bodies.

And so it was with Oliver. Every once in a while, the Miracle Man seemed a bit sluggish. At such times, Ollie simply chose to attend to business in the morning and then retreat to a large dog bed in the kitchen. No extra sniffing of the air or cruising down to the back gate—just "three downs and out" to use the football jargon. And late at night on his last walk of the day, Oliver sometimes was in no mood for any extracurricular activities; once again, business to be attended to and then up to the big bed for the night.

After a long streak of days marked by small but steady steps forward, those occasions were a gentle reminder that one day we will all stand face-to-face with our own mortality. The brief pauses in his progress offered a time to reflect on the fact that Ollie's pocketful of miracles would ultimately not include stiff-arming Father Time forever. There had been—and would continue to be—a noble effort to squeeze as much as possible out of the remaining days of his life, but the count of days would eventually be a finite tally. In the meantime, we were content to cherish each day, and Father Time was content simply to lurk in the shadows.

I found it impossible to watch my best friend in the midst of a showdown with his mortality without occasionally thinking about the one I would ultimately face with my own. Having escaped from that showdown several times in the past had no doubt steeled me for that moment—I had visited the cusp of that shadowy realm before but never become a citizen. The curious combination of my own history of medical trauma and a measure of financial security for my family—strange bedfellows indeed—had somehow enabled me to be philosophical about my own death. And yet I had shown more vulnerability to the prospect of Oliver's than I could possibly have imagined two months before.

But this was not a time for maudlin moments. It was a time for renewal and regeneration. While all the focus of attention had been on Oliver's physical condition, I had totally neglected my own. After a two-month hiatus, I literally jumped back into the pool to resume my daily regimen of vigorous laps in the early morning hours. Ever since Ollie's ICU experience, I hadn't had the willpower or the inclination to dive back into the bracing water and swim those laps before the crack of dawn. I certainly could have blamed my dereliction of exercise duty on my preoccupation with Ollie's condition or the formidable heap of business and photo projects that had piled up and buried my calendar in the process. But I don't think that was the real reason. In my somewhat rickety emotional state in the first few weeks after ICU, I had managed to delude myself into thinking that all my physical resources needed to be dedicated to supporting Oliver's struggle. At a time when I most needed the invigoration of regular exercise, I had allowed my aquatic regime to slip out of its well-worn groove.

I love swimming. After years of competing in high school and college, swimming comes naturally to me. And it affords my head the almost Zen-like experience of being dunked underwater where the extraneous sounds that normally disrupt thought are silenced. It offers a sensual retreat from the world at large into one of my own choosing.

For the first time in more than two months, I felt like swimming once again. And when at last my head was underwater and all I could hear was the gentle rush of water flowing past my outstretched body, I realized that there was indeed some connection between Ollie's return to his more normal routine and me to mine. Oliver had inched his way some distance from the edge of the precipice, and while that cliff was still visible in our rear-view mirror, it was time for me to resume a more normal approach to life as well. It was Day 71—and it was time to jump back in the pool.

Chapter Seventeen

Just a Pinch of Immortality

Days 72-78

EVERYONE DESERVES A DAY OF BEAUTY EVERY once in a while, and we figured that the Miracle Man was no exception. In the ten weeks since his discharge from ICU, Oliver had not once visited the tony canine salon Clip 'n Dip. Our boy was beginning to resemble the "dust mop" that a rather rude spectator at a horse show many years ago had likened him to. We were a bit anxious dropping Oliver off for a few hours, but the manager of Clip 'n Dip swore that hands and eyes would never be taken off him.

The entire clan had been customers of Clip 'n Dip for several years. So through tidings conveyed during recent appointments with his clan mates, the staff was already well versed on the drama of Ollie's medical crisis and recovery. When Oliver walked through the salon door propelled by his two front legs and his two back wheels, the entire assembled staff broke into raucous applause accompanied by chants of "Ollie! . . . Ollie! . . . Ollie!" (so familiar to boxing aficionados for whom the sound is spelled "Ali! . . . Ali!"). Never one to squander a dramatic moment, Oliver raced forward in his scooter and executed a series of pirouettes that would have been the envy of Baryshnikov. Ollie clearly knew the place, sensed the mood of the crowd, and realized that the moment was his to seize.

Two hours later, the Miracle Man emerged—the shears and shampoo of Clip 'n Dip had somehow managed to turn back the hands of time a notch or two. With a shorter, more precise coiffure, Ollie looked half his age. When I first saw him, I was confronted with overwhelming proof of what the matriarch of the Haas family knew so well: with a bit of primping and a talented hairdresser, the look of youth could always be restored to an uncanny degree.

Fresh on the heels of Oliver's day of beauty, Candice and I left town once again, this time for just over one week of teaching and the opening of an exhibit of my photo work at Yale. We had booked a bungalow at a quaint retreat tucked in the woods of central Connecticut, accessible to campus via a serpentine route through the New England countryside. On a day off from the lecture circuit, I headed over to the inn's swimming pool for my underwater constitutional. En route, I found myself chatting with one of the inn's attendants, singing the praises of this bucolic throwback to Revolutionary War days, my only lament being the "no pets" policy that had kept our clan at bay. One thing led to another, and soon I was relating the story of Oliver's past few months—the fall, the paralysis, the lung disease, the oxygen chamber, the rehab sessions, and the road to recovery.

As the attendant listened to this saga unfold, I noticed that she had become mesmerized by the twists and turns in Oliver's tale. And when I said, "Oliver is my best friend— truly my best friend," her eyes actually started to tear up and I felt a distinct lump in my throat. We were both caught off guard. I found it strange that I had abandoned my typical cloak of privacy that offered shelter from the prying eyes of others, and the attendant found herself moved to tears in the presence of a total stranger describing a crisis in his love affair with a dog she had never met.

When I saw firsthand the impact on a person who knew nothing of our lifelong bond until that very moment, it dawned on me just how powerful this tale of kinship truly was. I didn't delude myself into thinking that my relationship with Oliver was necessarily any closer or more loving than many thousands of other human-dog bonds out there. But I also realized that it was the very *non-uniqueness* of the tale—the fact that so many other people and so many other "Olivers" can form this cross-species bridge—that compelled its telling.

Told often enough, stories become tales and tales become legends . . . and if they are passed down from one generation to the next, those legends may live forever. All that is needed at the outset is a gripping tale, a universal theme that serves as the connecting thread, and a storyteller who is willing to open the cloak of privacy and share his innermost emotions. Once you have that within your grasp, you stand an outside chance of magically instilling your story and your protagonist with the most precious ingredient in the recipe of a life well lived—a pinch of immortality.

Perhaps through the filter of love that I placed over the lens of my mind—as with all filters that bend and shape the light—I was convinced during the nightmare in ICU that somewhere deep inside Oliver was an urging or an instinct that said, "I am not ready to die yet." This is pure speculation—it is all the musings of a man in love with a dog. And yet, perhaps that is exactly the point. Perhaps our feelings of love—be they for another person or an animal—allow us to translate what may be mundane events with a lexicon that no one else may have and see meanings that no one else quite does. One of the great beauties of love is that in the end, no one is in a position to contradict our impressions when we see the object of our affections as beautiful or noble or brilliant.

I will never know for sure what went through Oliver's mind in ICU. All I do know is that his rally back to life from the low point in that oxygen chamber is consistent with what I ascribed to Oliver as the determination not to allow his life to end at that point. And it was that very determination that became the kernel of the legend of the Miracle Man. His emergence from intensive care and the partial recovery from his paralysis—standing on all fours, scooting around in his chariot, taking a few steps unaided by man or device—all enhanced the legend. And when I saw the impact of his story on a total stranger at a retreat in the woods of Connecticut, I felt both a sense of pride in Oliver and a belief that the legend imbued him with just a pinch of immortality.

Chapter Eighteen

The Toast of the Town

Days 79-82

ON THE LAST DAY OF MY BRIEF TEACHING sabbatical at Yale, Candice and I were treated to another upbeat report from my assistant, Christine, who had accompanied Oliver to his weekly rehab session: an impressive twenty-five sit-to-stand reps with no support from his therapist and sixteen straight minutes of trotting in the tank, highlighted by his right rear leg (the laggard to date) keeping pace with his left on the underwater treadmill. With the benefit of the buoyancy offered by the water, Oliver had progressed to the point where there was some four-legged walking in the tank at every therapy session.

What was critical at this stage of recovery was not whether Oliver would ever regain full use of his back legs, but rather the fact that there was steady improvement in his movement and some healing of his spinal cord—it was the direction and not the magnitude of the changes that was heartening. Whether Ollie ever walked normally again had become secondary in my mind. Of greater significance was the fact that he was not deteriorating the way most fourteen-year-olds do.

Oliver was offering a tutorial in a course in which I had yet to achieve any grade higher than an Incomplete. The course would have been titled "Managing Lofty Expectations—How to Lower the Bar." I was learning how to place his achievements in context—and the context in which his progress was remarkable was in direct comparison with what his situation had been in ICU, not with what "might have been" before his tumble down that embankment. Alive was better than dying . . . partially mobile was better than not mobile at all . . . aging gracefully was better than falling apart overnight. I had learned to manage my expectations about him, and perhaps that would one day be a guide in learning how to manage my expectations about myself. After all, it might not be such a stretch to apply the lessons learned from an alpha male to an alpha personality. In any event, his progress was cause for celebration, and I was at least learning how to celebrate.

There was further cause for celebration of a different sort on the last night in New Haven. After attending the opening of my photo exhibit at the recently renovated Yale Art & Architecture Complex, two close business colleagues of mine from Wall Street, Martín and Kevin, together with our wives and a few friends, retreated to the restaurant Ibiza for world-class Hispanic cuisine to mark the exhibit festivities.

Early on in the dinner, Martín and Kevin inquired as to Oliver's recovery. There was no need to review the history of the tumble in California or his stay in ICU—both men had been kept abreast of his situation via a steady stream of e-mails during the rough days in intensive care and the first few weeks of home care thereafter. Even though there was always a cluster of tasks on our collective plates, it was a rare e-mail from either fellow that did not open or close with an inquiry about Oliver's health. In the course of working together in the trenches, we had all become sensitive to what was critical to each other.

Over dinner, I recounted with the pride of a beaming father Oliver's exploits in his new wheels and his overall sense of well-being. As I did so, I noted in Kevin's and Martín's expressions a genuine delight with the detailed account of his recovery. The emotional bond that Ollie and I shared had clearly registered with my cohorts. Others might have viewed the three of us as wily veterans of the hard-nosed games played on Wall Street who rarely opened up their softer side—but we knew differently. Kevin and Martín had a very clear idea as to where Oliver ranked in my universe. Their expressions of concern throughout the past eighty days—and again that night—were both heartfelt and touching.

At the end of the update, I concluded by saying, "Someday you guys will meet Oliver." At precisely the same moment, Kevin and Martín raised their glasses and, as if on cue, said in unison, "We would welcome that." I was struck by both the fact that the toast had been offered in tandem and also by such a simple and genteel phrase—*we would welcome that*. The upraised glasses and the promise of a meeting one day were something very special—Oliver was indeed the toast of the town that night.

Ollie may have been the toast of the town in New Haven, but New Haven was not his town—Dallas was his town, and it was time to return home. Once we arrived back in Dallas the next morning, the guys offered up a rambunctious display of affection—even Chloe dropped her normal coyness in favor of a few pirouettes and a quivering behind. After a brief session of group groping in the kitchen and a *lacka-walka* for his younger brothers, I decided that the clan leader deserved his own spin outside, figuring that would entail just a few minutes of leisurely strolling up and down the driveway.

But Oliver had something else in mind. From the moment we wheeled out the front door, he headed straight for the furthest edge of the property and then proceeded to march around the entire perimeter of our homestead, including a circumnavigation of the small lake and passage over two footbridges. I felt as if Oliver were deliberately extending our private time together to the absolute maximum. Along the way, he even made a headlong charge at a gaggle of mallard ducks, who escaped to the safe haven of the lake to avoid this half-bicycle, half-canine predator. Ollie left no doubt in the minds of those quacking interlopers that nothing on our property was beyond his limits and that this was still his turf. It was indeed an impressive display.

After grabbing Oliver in his scooter before the momentum of his duck-charge catapulted him over the edge of the lake embankment into the drink, I chuckled at his bravado. Apparently, there was nothing inherent in his physical condition that was about to derail him from the notion that his position as clan leader was inviolate and his duty to chase trespassers off our property was sacrosanct.

Once Oliver calmed down from Operation Mallard and ceased barking at the disbanded flock, we headed back home together—but I thought about that duck-charge some more. It may have been just a brief interlude of instinct, a dog chasing a few birds. But perhaps it was also the perfect metaphor for what I was learning from Oliver—a physically challenged dog not feeling sorry for himself but accepting his limitations without handing over his dignity to the weight of his infirmities. An aging veteran no longer able to run with the abandon of youth but still willing to protect his turf against unwelcome intruders—compromising only on what was possible physically but not on his principles.

Ollie was not the only veteran on the walk that afternoon—there was another one at the other end of the leash. Another who would inevitably face his own physical decline at some point and would need to decide which ducks were worth chasing and which were not.

Chapter Nineteen

Respect for Our Elders

Days 83-88

ONLY ABOUT TWO WEEKS BEFORE OLIVER AND I reached the one-hundred-day mark, I attended my first Orthodox Jewish wedding. A combination of unrestrained festivities and rigid traditions baked over a period of two thousand years, the millennia-old religious ceremonies were balanced in equal measure against the modernity of blaring music and wild dancing.

Normally after an evening with a throng of people (virtually none of whom I had ever met before), the kaleidoscope of images I had absorbed would evaporate within minutes of walking through the exit. But two images from that night would stick in my mind for quite a while. One was that of an older Orthodox man seated directly in front of me scrolling around a handheld device throughout the entire service. At first, I thought this gentleman had somehow inscribed the words of the ceremony on his device and was following along with the invocations by the long sequence of rabbis who took turns at the microphone in this marathon service. When I leaned forward and looked over his shoulder, I was surprised to learn that his intense concentration on the PDA was due to playing, over and over again, a game that closely resembled the Pac-Man classic from the Stone Age of video games.

The other image that would resonate even longer was a gesture of deep respect paid to the elderly. As the wedding processional unfolded, the surviving grandparents of first the groom and then the bride walked down the center aisle, alone and unassisted. As each octogenarian shuffled past the rows of seated Orthodox, the men all rose and bowed in a gesture of respect for their elders. It was a touching moment, one of those cherished traditions that has unfortunately slipped away in many cultures—a visible nod of respect to those who have reached the final arc of their life path.

At that moment, I thought of our daughter Vanessa and the wedding in Turks & Caicos that was only a few months away. On the cusp of the marriage of one of your children—particularly a father's youngest daughter—the conventional thinking is that you obsess on how time has just whizzed by and the baby that you diapered a few decades ago has evolved into a woman "in the blink of an eye." While I had traces of that thought, it was not the one that came to mind that night. I rarely focused on Vanessa's evolution from birth to age twenty-seven, but often tried to visualize her continuing development from age twenty-seven on—into middle age and beyond. I long ago accepted the fact that Vanessa had passed through childhood and puberty and young womanhood—it was a natural progression and I had been there every step of the way. But the realization that Vanessa would one day be in her fifties and sixties and even beyond was considerably more daunting—for the simple reason that I would not be there every step of the way. The thought that I was about to hand Vanessa off to Gavin at the end of a walk down the wooden pier to the beach at our retreat in Parrot Cay was thrilling and wholly expected—but the thought that she might one day reprise the scene at that Orthodox wedding and walk down the center aisle as an octogenarian grandmother of the bride or groom was simply overwhelming.

At that moment, I also thought of Oliver. I thought of him walking down that wooden pier to the beach where Vanessa and Gavin would soon be married. I envisioned the assembled crowd standing as one and bowing to his noble efforts to pull his harnessed chariot through the sand that will surround the exact spot of their exchanging vows. I thought of how touched I would feel by his presence at that moment, when the thirteen-year-old girl who helped rescue him from a no-kill shelter would begin the process of starting her own family. And I thought of our bowing to this aging leader of an aging clan, showing our respect for his having negotiated the long path to that spot on the beach where we would celebrate the fresh bonds of the young and pay our respects to the old.

A voyage down uncharted roads—on life paths or in lands that you have never experienced before—inevitably changes you. And usually it's for the better, since the insights that are gained along the way afford a different angle from which to view the much smaller world that you normally inhabit.

The trek beside Oliver had been no exception. On this journey, I had learned to pay attention to the details of what surrounded me. In the course of my studying Oliver ever so meticulously to detect any changes in his behavior or his vitals, I noticed things that were directly in front of my eyes but had somehow not registered before. I began to focus more closely on a process that had left center stage for the moment but would inevitably return to claim the starring role—the visible traces of his aging.

The most conspicuous sign of that process was his coat. Except for the white goatee, white chest, and two white socks at the bottom of his back legs that had adorned his body ever since birth, this once black-and-white puppy was now covered almost completely in gray. Black had been mostly replaced by gray, but Oliver had obviously stayed entirely within the black-white-gray family of colors. I thought from time to time that an image of Oliver taken with color film would be virtually indistinguishable from one taken in black-and-white.

By staying within this monochromatic zone, Oliver had preserved—or perhaps enhanced—a certain melancholy that resonates from images cast in black-and-white alone. When I was on photo safaris in Africa, each time I reached inside my vest pocket, I had a choice that our photographic ancestors of the 1940s and 1950s never did—I had to decide whether to load a roll of color or black-and-white film into the back of the camera body. It was a decision that would frame the story I hoped to tell about the tiny slice of time and space that I would capture on film that day.

Monochromatic film is a medium with its own unique properties that will never be banished to the proverbial dustbin of history alongside the buggy whip and the rotary phone. For reasons that may forever remain a mystery, black-and-white has the uncanny ability, despite its chromatic limitations, to evoke a more emotive, more poignant, and often more meaningful reaction in the viewer. Even the grainy, imprecise cast of old photographs of mine workers or Confederate soldiers with frozen faces and ramrod straight posture delivers an emotional punch that could hardly be duplicated in color. The seventy-year-old photograph of a clean-shaven aviator posing beside his aircraft lends a measure of dignity to my father's image that color could not possibly duplicate, an image immune from fair comparison with the red splotches and blue varicose veins that littered the landscape of the eighty-eight-year-old's face at the time of his passing.

Oliver's gray-and-white palette has also shown the ability to deliver that emotional punch—there is a certain dignity and melancholy that emanates from my most recent photographic and mental images of Oliver. Those qualities are perhaps most evident in his face, where the faraway look in his cataract-filled eyes seems to focus Oliver's attention on a world that we could hardly imagine, let alone see.

When I would study the details in Oliver's fourteen-year-old face, I was reminded of a ballad sung by Willie Nelson that exalts the way in which the years have etched their tracks across his face and those lines had become like old friends. Willie has shown the uncanny ability to march in step with time, to allow the travails that have pockmarked his life to be absorbed into his skin and yet leave his disposition none the worse for wear. The voice has taken on more gravel, but not lost its soothing timbre; the braided ponytails have ceded their color to gray, but not lost their charming defiance; and that face—that deeply furrowed, leather-beaten face—has lost its youth but none of its appeal. The years have not robbed Willie of classic beauty—his vault of riches never warehoused that wasting asset. Somehow, Willie has managed to grow older without growing old.

As in Willie's case, time has not yet learned how to ravage the grace and dignity in Oliver's distinguished visage—and this ability to deny the reality of the clock is rare indeed. Time is a patient master of its game, able to dethrone even the most heavenly bodies and the most vibrant minds. The aging process—so often coupled with debilitating disease—is ultimately a cruel trick that awaits almost all those who dare enter the latter stages of a long life. The "Ali shuffle" that blinded ringside observers with its dazzling speed in the sixties has been reduced to a heart-wrenching shuffle in slow motion by an icon for the ages.

Is this the destiny that awaits us all, save those who are spared its indignities by an "early" death? Are we condemned to a time when our children will bathe our ruined bodies and chaperone the purging of waste from our systems? The prospect is enough to shield our eyes in a painful wince.

Whenever I witnessed death in the wilds of Africa, it was a sobering experience—sobering but not depressing, for death in that venue is so often shrouded in a certain dignity and purpose. A fleet-footed impala brought down by a sprinting cheetah has lived its final moments in a race between titans; an aging lion who succumbs to the challenge of another who would be king has come full circle, doubling back on the time when he soared to the head of the pride by overthrowing his predecessor; even a young zebra taken in the jaws of a croc that explodes from beneath the surface of the water has prolonged the life of a species that traces its roots to the age of dinosaurs. I never felt that time had played a cruel trick on those creatures, whose lives were ended in order that others could survive. Those are the rules of the game in the wild. Life is not long out there, but time rarely saps the dignity of the players on that stage. It does not gradually deflate a once-proud body until what remains barely resembles what once was there.

I have often photographed the face of an aging lion. I am fascinated by the history written beneath its eyes and across its forehead, the scores of cuts and gouges and scars that are the souvenirs of a lifetime of confrontation—but also the mementos of an existence lived to the fullest, the hallmarks of a body that has managed to weave its way along the narrow precipice that separates survival from extinction. As I would stare into an aging lion's amber eyes, I could almost hear the words of this noble creature echo those of the ballad sung by Willie Nelson, lamenting the fact that the marks upon its face are like old friends.

And when I stared at the details in Oliver's face, I could see the same nobility that I saw in that lion's eyes, the same wisdom that has been accumulated from a long trail of life experiences, and the same acceptance of the march of time without the agony of those who expect to cheat death. In the course of this one-hundred-day journey, I have learned a great deal from the Miracle Man—about respect for our elders and about aging with dignity. It is a lesson that will come in handy one day—when I stare into the mirror and see that the lines beneath my eyes are like old friends.

Chapter Twenty

Oliver's Cove

Days 89-100

"What lies behind us and what lies before us are tiny matters compared to what lies within us."
—Oliver Wendell Holmes

IT WAS ONLY FITTING THAT THE ONE-HUNDRED-day journey should end where I had dreamt it would—at Oliver's Cove. In the midst of one of the bleakest days in ICU, when there was no response in Oliver's vacant eyes, I would still try to get a message through to him. I would lean forward, place my head inside the oxygen chamber, lift one of his drooping ears, and whisper a few words slowly and softly in a rhythm that allowed Ollie to recollect that it was "his Bobby" at the other end and that the message was a good one. The words I whispered were "One day we will walk that beach again."

One day we will walk that beach again . . . When I first whispered that phrase, the thought of our walking together on a distant beach was a flight of fancy that existed in my mind alone. It was a promise I shared with no one but Oliver, since everyone else was concerned with his surviving just one day at a time. And while I never allowed my own doubts to infect the whispered message, the thought in my mind was more along the lines of *What I wouldn't give for just one more walk along that beach with you.* Those few minutes of whispering and withdrawing and then thinking about that beach were exquisitely painful . . . but with just a trace of hope attached to that distant goal.

"That beach" is a pristine stretch of sand along the edge of a tiny island called Parrot Cay in the British West Indies where we have a beach home. There are just a few other homes on the island—a spit of sand that rises up from the ocean with marshes on one side and salt-white sand edging turquoise waters on the other. No roads, no stores, no visitors other than those who stay for a few days in a small resort at the other end of the island.

It is the place where years ago Ollie and I began our tradition of walking the beach every morning. In the old days, we would stroll through the water, listen to the light surf, and talk to each other, one of us out loud and the other through his eyes. When we walked the beach at Parrot Cay, Oliver set a slower pace for the two of us—literally and figuratively.

Although I attached a leash to his collar, it was only for the purpose of tugging him gently through the particularly deep hillocks of sand or clumps of seaweed we encountered when we drifted far from the water's edge. Along the flat surface of beach, I neither strained on the leash nor did Ollie—it hung limply between our bodies. We did not race or jog; we ambled at a very slow and steady pace, one that allowed thoughts to drift in and out with the cadence of the waves. It was one of the few places in the world—and one of the only times—that I would allow my chronically restless mind to fall in sync with our deliberate gait.

We continued the tradition even after Oliver was no longer able to see the waves break but could still hear the surf pound—even after a leash was needed to prevent him from bumping into the sharp edges of driftwood that would occasionally wash up on the beach. Ollie's eventual lack of sight was a neutral here, for there was almost no one to see or anything to disturb the endlessness of the sand or the constancy of the ocean. Even after his sight deserted him, the walk still meant the same—perhaps even more, since I knew full well that our days there were numbered.

Even then, I realized that this regular morning walk would one day become an image that would come to mind whenever we could no longer walk together. There would never come a time when I stared at that beach without seeing him romp in the waters—the light waves along the shore would never completely erase his paw prints in the sand.

When our daughter, Vanessa, decided that she would be married there, on the beach at sunset, we wanted to have an address to inscribe on the wedding invitation for our small island retreat, and so it became *Oliver's Cove*, forever memorializing his attachment to his favorite haunt, and mine to him.

Oliver's Cove was all I ever wanted in a home—ever since I was homeless almost fifty years ago. It was neither large nor elaborate, and it was built with the fruits of a business career that offered far more reward than entitlement. For me, it had always been a retreat in every sense of the word—an asylum, a haven, a sanctuary, a shelter, a place to withdraw to. We built this place on what was a vacant clump of raw sand, and it was constructed only to please its occupants and not to impress others—for others were rarely to be found on this nearly peopleless island.

It was a bricks-and-mortar reflection of my aerial photography, a lifting away from the sanity—and the insanity—of my other life. It was the anti–Wall Street, a locale where currency had no place and prestige had no meaning. It was the venue where the things that I learned to trust the least in life had no valid passport for entry. And for Oliver, it was a place to be cherished just as passionately. For him, it was where "his Bobby" spent virtually the entire time with him and never left for days on end, and where strangers almost never came to call and challenge the perimeter of his domain. It was a place where I had never said good-bye to Oliver . . . or Oliver to me. It was a place where I could not help but walk around all day and breathe in air that was rarified with the gift of good fortune and expel breath infused with gratitude for the gift of being there.

Almost one hundred days before, when I first whispered a promise that I was not sure I could keep, this island became the Holy Grail of our odyssey. It became the destination of that long march in which memories of ICU would fade away and the white sand beaches up ahead would become a reality.

In the last few days before our winter break, when the family would converge on the islet of Parrot Cay, I was nearly giddy with anticipation that Oliver and I would soon plant our feet on that beach in what had become our Promised Land. Over and over again, I would whisper a very different message in Ollie's ears—this time it was, "We're going to Parrot Cay . . . Parrot Cay!!!" I didn't delude myself into thinking that Oliver could possibly find that tiny island on a map of the British West Indies or even point to the broad expanse of the Caribbean. But I wasn't counting on his skills as a cartographer—I was banking on his prowess as a listener and on the fact that the simple phrase "We're going to Parrot Cay" had been uttered so many times before and had always elicited a very tangible form of anticipation—a pricking up of the ears, a bark of recognition, and an impatient wagging tail.

Simple phrases—*time for a lacka-walka . . . your Bobby's home . . . we're going to Parrot Cay*—eventually registered in the boys' minds, not with the exact comprehension we humans ascribed to the words but at a level that would convey a reasonable facsimile of the intended meaning. The keys to delivering the message were repetition, a certain number of syllables, and a cadence with a distinct lift in the voice at the end. We could easily have substituted a different location at the end of the phrase so long as it rhymed with "Parrot Cay" (Cay pronounced "key")—we might just as well have said, "We're going to Wounded Knee . . . Wounded Knee!!!" and Ollie would have figured a good place awaited our departure. But no such word games were employed this time around. It was a simple, straightforward "We're going to Parrot Cay!!!" Occasionally for good measure, I would add: "No way we're not going to make it now, Ollie . . . no way, man!!!"

On the day before our departure, we packed up all the necessary canine accoutrements for a two-week stay on the island—cartons of dog food, medications for each of the guys bundled in separate Ziploc pouches, stuffed animals and other assorted toys, Ollie's chariot, his Harley-Davidson baseball cap, a tangle of leashes, and all the other paraphernalia that could possibly be needed over the break—since there were no grocery stores or vet's office on the island.

The actual trek down to Parrot Cay is a logistical obstacle course—roughly five hours of flight time terminating on the main island of Providenciales, followed by the immigration authorities' slow-motion review of human passports and canine medical certificates, then a long van ride to the dock on the other side of Provo, and finally a forty-minute boat ride to the small dock on Parrot Cay. Once we arrived at the beach house, what often ensued was a wrestling match with some combination of mechanical malfunctions that had sprung up since our last visit—an air conditioner that would no longer hum, a telephone line that greeted us with utter silence, an Internet connection that refused to acknowledge that the twenty-first century had in fact arrived. Candice would normally attend to the non-computer glitches, while I would obsessively attempt to restore my Internet lifeline to the outside world. It was almost as if the technological greeting that we often received upon arrival was a deliberate set-up—a clever scheme orchestrated by some mystical force—designed to instill a greater sense of appreciation for the days of R&R that lay ahead. On this particular trip, the Internet connection was exceedingly obstinate and, after a few hours of hand-to-hand combat, it grudgingly allowed a slow form of access that we hoped would gain a bit more traction in the days ahead.

By the time the technological hurdles had been cleared, the prolonged travel had taken its toll on the clan, and all the guys were out for the count—doing a good imitation of furry throw rugs in the kitchen. But a mere case of exhaustion was not about to stave off the triumphant beach walk that Oliver and I had planned in ICU what seemed like ages ago. I woke Ollie up from his deep slumber, hitched his slumping body to the scooter, and carried him over the steps that lead to the outside decking. I thought Ollie might be too exhausted to actually walk the beach, so we just sat at the end of the pier and listened to the surf—for all of about one minute. Oliver started to wriggle and almost jumped off the edge of the pier down to the beach, a distance of only about twelve inches but still not advisable when you're strapped into a scooter. Ollie tossed me a defiant look, and I could just about read his thin black lips exclaiming, "Dad, we're here to walk the beach, not sit on some damn pier!" So off we went.

And the years just melted away. As soon as those wheels hit the hard part of the beach where the waves had just flattened the sand, Ollie was on his way. We blazed a trail all the way down to where rocky extensions prevented further ambling at high tide, then reversed course and headed home. Along the way, Ollie marked his turf with two torpedoes that we covered with mounds of sand, thereby creating the beach equivalent of land mines. It was a day—and a walk—that marked a goal we had set more than three months before when intravenous tubes and heart monitors connected Ollie to the world of the living—and when storming the beaches at Parrot Cay was hardly more than a distant mirage. Instead of simply declining gracefully into old age, the post-tumble Oliver had taken a U-turn on the highway to aging—our boy had spun gold out of rotting straw and come up with a new stage in his life that had restored his youthful vigor.

Even though we had not quite reached the one-hundred-day mark, we had arrived on Parrot Cay . . . at the newly named Oliver's Cove. At the end of that walk, I could feel my chest deflate as all the tension of pursuing a long-sought-after destination escaped. I had rarely allowed myself the luxury of that feeling before—perhaps when I closed a cluster of deals that vaulted lifelong ambitions to within my grasp, or when my first book with National Geographic was released after years of intense focus on the minute details of images and words that were the survivors of endless rounds of editing. At rare times like that, my feelings were a delicious blend of relief and pride—I wouldn't know whether to laugh or cry, so in a moment of total privacy, I would do a bit of both, allowing a faint smile to crease my cheeks as I would wipe away a few tears that escaped my best efforts to keep them in my eyes. I did both that day with Oliver—I smiled and I cried, and both felt awfully good.

By the time we bedded down for our first night on the island, I knew that nothing could derail the inevitability of our completing this one-hundred-day journey. We were less than two weeks away and were ensconced at our safe-haven, our refuge, our ultimate destination. All that remained was the passage of time, the flip of a few more days on a December calendar that was running out of pages. At the end of this marathon, no interloper was about to snatch from our hands the flag that signified triumph during our leisurely victory lap around the stadium. The finale to our journey could not have been designed more perfectly. With just a handful of days to go before the ultimate one hundred, we had time to savor in small gulps the sweet taste of arriving at our goal.

We found comfort in the fact that each day on the island bore a remarkable resemblance to the one before. At night, after watching the psychedelic sunsets that the Caribbean has to offer, we were content to retire to the big bed—filled from stem to stern with the inert bodies of a clan of dogs and a pair of humans—and rest up before the challenge of another day without challenges.

In an effort to clear the detritus of work out of the way each morning before the boys stretched their way out of a long night's snooze, I would arise even earlier than normal— in the realm of 4:00 a.m.—so that by breakfast, the coast was almost totally clear. The fact that Wall Street traditionally begins its annual winter hibernation no later than mid-December provided a serendipitous lull in the storm of my business life, as colleagues from the canyons of Manhattan had similarly scattered to the four winds in a temporary diaspora of investment moguls.

Our days were exceedingly simple—my early morning swim . . . hours wiled away with a few of the boys competing for space between my outstretched legs . . . a Corona with lime every afternoon . . . walks with Candice back and forth on the beach with several four-leggers in tow. Each day was punctuated by a few feats from Oliver, such as a prolonged stand with his gray hair ruffled by the wind.

But of course, the highlights of my time with Ollie were our walks along the beach in his scooter, always one in the morning and normally another in the afternoon if the heat and humidity were not too oppressive for an elder gent in a fur coat. When I would drop his leash on those walks and allow him to amble at will, most often Oliver would approach the line where the last few mini-waves had left gentle creases in the sand—and then he would turn and face the ocean. For a minute or so at a time, Oliver would stand almost perfectly still, his back legs stretched out in his stirrups, his tail held high, and his head lifted proudly to catch the scents from the surface of the water. The only movement that I could detect was his nose twitching as if to decipher a stream of messages that paraded through his nostrils. I withdrew from him far enough not to be a distraction, but close enough to grab his chariot if a random high wave reared up. Oliver would stare out at the water and at the horizon. I was never quite sure what those eyes were taking in, but it hardly seemed to matter. At those moments, I may not have known what Oliver was seeing, but I knew exactly what I could see: the promise of the one hundred days about to be fulfilled, and an old soul at peace with himself and with the world.

It was also a time to pay tribute to the Miracle Man. It was a time to acknowledge that not all miracles in life are accompanied by fairy dust and magic wands. Sometimes miracles only need the carousel to stop spinning long enough for us to realize that simply being on that wooden horse is a marvelous ride in and of itself—a ride that we will dearly miss when the carnival shuts down and moves to another town.

At last Day 100 arrived, and we celebrated by reprising the serene antics of each of the prior days. In the late afternoon, Oliver and I headed out to the end of the pier and took our accustomed position, seated just a few feet apart on the deck facing the ocean, two travelers who had completed their odyssey together. It was a moment of exquisite triumph, and we had a cold bottle of Corona to symbolize our toast to each other. We had started off one hundred days before when this moment seemed somewhere between a pipe dream and a distant horizon. But as with all distant horizons that you relentlessly pursue, we had arrived at the point we had set our compass to.

At the time we staked out one hundred days as the ultimate goal of our journey, it seemed such an artificial number, chosen as an even-numbered compromise between being too close in to qualify as an odyssey and being so far out as to be greedy given Oliver's weakened condition. But like many other goals that pinpoint an artificial number, the one-hundred-day mark had somehow proven to be incredibly appropriate. Oliver had risen in strength and mobility to a plateau that still sloped gently upward—but one that was no longer close to the edge of the cliff.

With the Corona bottle sweating into my hand in the late afternoon sun, I thought about how the characters in this drama had adjusted their roles along the way. This journey had been conceived as a one-man play in which Oliver would be the only actor on stage and I would be his faithful companion. But the drama had noticeably changed along the way. Over time, Oliver's performance had drawn his companion closer and closer to center stage.

Simply witnessing his struggles and his progress had cast one of the floodlights in the orchestra on my own struggles and my own progress in overcoming those struggles. For indeed, regardless of age or circumstance or physical prowess, we all struggle, for that is the nature of life itself. And sometimes, when the outside world seems to think that "we have it all," the solution to the struggles becomes most inscrutable—for at that point, we have become isolated and have lost our ability to confide in others, who might not imagine that we too have our doubts and our challenges and our setbacks.

But I could always confide in Oliver—Oliver and his travails had become the mirror of what I felt inside on my strongest days and on the days when I could sense my own knees begin to buckle. Our linkage of spirit had become the thoroughfare for traveling down the road toward greater enlightenment. I had learned more in the past one hundred days from a nearly blind fourteen-year-old dog in a wheelchair than from all the great professors I had been privileged to listen to in the ivy-covered buildings of our finest universities. And the lectures did not need to take place in an amphitheater with seats that numbered in the hundreds—there was just one Professor and one disciple at opposite ends of a leash.

Epilogue

Falling in Love

Day 200

OLIVER CELEBRATED HIS TWO HUNDREDTH DAY following release from intensive care by instigating a brief scuffle with Henry, a bloodless confrontation in which the only casualty was Candice's ankle, which had somehow managed to come between a growling Henry and a lunging Oliver. The clan leader and his sidekick Elmer had just returned from a few days in Parrot Cay, and I suppose Ollie thought it necessary to remind Henry that his brief tenure as clan leader *pro tem* was over the moment Ollie set paw back on the Dallas property. It was not a fight for the ages but only a brief flashback to the time when Oliver and Henry would stage a battle every once in a while. While it left Candice wincing in pain for a few minutes, no skin was punctured and no blood flowed. The whole incident left me more convinced than ever that our boy would never concede the mantle of leadership to another. Despite all his infirmities and the fatigue of the seven-hour trip home from Parrot Cay, Ollie was spoiling for a chance to reassert his position as commander-in-chief.

I guess that's one of the reasons why I love Oliver the way I do. I love those who have an insatiable thirst to lead and know no other way. And I love the Jerry Lee Lewises of the world—the old rockers who defiantly refuse to leave the stage as long as they still have the power to pound out melodies on those ivories.

The past seven months with Oliver have proven to be a refresher course in the art of falling in love and being in love—and the difference between the two. Falling in love is easy; it's being in love that's the hard part. Falling in love is the emotional equivalent of skydiving. You hurl yourself out of an open aircraft, and all of a sudden you're just floating in the wide-open spaces with gravity exerting its inexorable tug upon your body. You assume a spread-eagle position with limbs extended and begin to spin with the currents that take control of your journey. You are untethered by any responsibilities and only too thrilled to keep falling as you hurtle toward earth.

But eventually it's time to land, so you tug at the cord to release the parachute that will break your fall. If it works, you land on terra firma and begin the tougher process of just being in love. Once your feet are planted firmly on the ground, you attempt to find your bearings, you place one foot in front of the other, and you resume a more normal life. As you unfasten the parachute, you strap on the cords of responsibility.

Normally, the process of falling in love and being in love is a sequential one—the falling precedes the being, and the two just barely overlap. But in the case of the past seven months with Oliver, I had managed to do both. Certainly, I had to keep my feet planted firmly on the ground at all times—alternately beset by his medical challenges and buoyed by small steps forward. The mundane responsibilities that bind a man to his dog were a part of my daily routine. But I also floated in the air as I luxuriated in Oliver's last-minute reprieve and the striking progress in his strength and mobility. We had borrowed a chunk of time from "what might have been" that kept us in that exhilarating free fall with our arms locked tightly around each other.

The sensation of falling in love is one thing, but the actual experience of falling down a cliff is something else again. I was totally unprepared for Oliver to fall off the edge of that embankment. For someone who craves order and precision as much as I do, Oliver's unscripted exit from my life would have been the very antithesis of the right-angled structure around which I had built my own sense of safety and security. I had been caught off guard and was no longer in control of events. What I needed more than anything else at that point was time—time to restore order, time to reconstruct my fractured plans, time to prepare myself for my best friend's eventual departure.

In the early part of our long journey together, I sometimes looked back at the narrow escape from death that Oliver had somehow engineered. But in the later days, I only looked forward toward that ever-closer milestone of the one hundredth day. By the end of the one hundred days, I neither looked forward nor back. I no longer dwelt upon the past, nor did I preoccupy myself with the future. We had been granted the wish that we had wished for—our one hundred days together. It was a fair bargain. Once we passed that milestone, I never forgot that I was in the gravy zone—that every additional day was more than we had bargained for.

Occasionally, my thoughts drift toward the inevitable time when Oliver will be separated from my day-to-day life. But those thoughts are fleeting and are easily banished from my mind. Instead, I notice how I take absolutely nothing for granted now with him or with any of his clan mates. When I wake up each morning, I no longer spring out of bed drawn by the aroma of that first cup of coffee and the compulsion of the tasks on my to-do list. I linger for a while among those furry bodies and stroke anyone who happens to be within reach— which always includes Oliver. Moment to moment, I am more aware of his love for me and of mine for him. Whenever we are together, I am better able to cast off the distracting thoughts that normally clutter my mind and instead focus on Ollie. When I walk with him, I am inclined to let his leash go slack and not cut short our time together simply because

I have a conference call coming up or photos that need to be reviewed. Everything takes its place behind Oliver during our moments together—I figure there will be plenty of time for those other things at some point.

In every sense of the word, Oliver is continuing to make further strides. His latest rehab session was another record-breaker—five continuous minutes of unassisted standing on all fours, as well as twenty vigorous minutes in the hydrotherapy tank including several when his rear legs would take full strides in sync with his front. Last night in bed, even on the soft and lumpy mattress, Oliver managed to lift himself up to a standing position and shuffle forward a few steps.

Our life together continues to unfold one day at a time, and it is so much more than just "more time" together. The moments are nothing short of exquisite—Oliver is exceedingly content, I am exceedingly content, and we are exceedingly content to be together still.